Catch a Falling Star

Thief of Hearts Series   Book II

Mason Stone

Dedicated to the Goddess of Love, and her merry helpers.

And to Pig--my one and only.

© 2019 Red Pine Publishing, Toronto, Canada
All rights reserved.

Cover image courtesy Jonny Lindner from Pixabay

<u>Disclaimer</u>
This is a work of fiction, and all persons are fictional. Certain place names have been used to give verisimilitude to the text. Any resemblance to real persons and events are purely coincidental.

Keep up with news at:
http://perryisnormal.blogspot.ca

PART ONE   BY CHANCE   5

Chapter One   I Met Him At The Corner   5

Chapter Two   Bitter Medicine   19

Chapter Three   What Are Friends For?   34

Chapter Four   Tangled   52

Chapter Five   Kiss and Tell   62

PART TWO   BY CIRCUMSTANCE   82

Chapter Six   New Year's Resolutions   82

Chapter Seven   Ups and Downs   99

Chapter Eight   Danger Ahead!   132

Chapter Nine   More Creepy   154

Chapter Ten   A Birthday Surprise   176

Chapter Eleven   Close To You   184

PART THREE   BY CHOICE   197

Chapter Twelve   Close Calls   197

Chapter Thirteen   Two Steps Forward   214

Chapter Fourteen   One Step Back   227

Chapter Fifteen   No Safe Haven   238

Chapter Sixteen	Is there a Plan B?	254
Chapter Seventeen	Make Or Break	264
Chapter Eighteen	California Dreaming	272

PART ONE   BY CHANCE

Chapter One   I Met Him At The Corner

It was a Tuesday, and Marlee McCowan was late for her appointment. When you are late, even the slight traffic congestion in a smaller city can be frustrating. Spokane did not get anything like the rain that Seattle did, but it could make the street quite slippery.

Turning the corner, her eye just caught something, and it was moving into her path and not giving her time to compute what exactly it was.

Instinctively, she swerved to avoid the dog, but could not miss its owner who rushed out-- perhaps to save the animal from harm.

The man was down and the dog stood over him, wagging his tail, knowing something was wrong here.

Marlee braked to a stop and pulled to the side of the street that led to the hospital where the interview team was waiting. She was going to have to be late.

"I'm so sorry. Are you hurt? Where does it hurt?"

The dog licked her hand as she stood over the man, who had now rolled onto his back but had not gotten to his feet.

"It's my fault," he said. "I ran after my dog; I wasn't thinking."

"No, I wasn't focused on driving. Let me call 9-1-1," she said.

"What's your dog's name?" Marlee said lamely.
What do you say right after you run someone down?

"Ripley. He's my buddy, aren't you, Rip?" He stroked the dog's chest and pulled his head into his own. Then he winced.

"Something's broken. My side hurts and it hurts to move my arms."

Just then, the ambulance rolled up, and two paramedics jumped out to attend to him. They told him to stay flat, as they palpated his chest, arms, and legs for obvious signs of injury.

"Okay, pal, let's get you onto a stretcher and in to the E.R. Just stay quiet."

Marlee watched anxiously as they lifted and slid him into the vehicle.

"Wait! What's your name?"

"Daniel. Daniel Briar. What's yours?"

"Marlee. Look, I'm sorry. I will come and we can talk. I'll find you. I know this hospital pretty well. I'm an intern there."

She wanted to touch him. But the medics hustled him in and slammed the doors.

The vehicle disappeared down 8th Avenue with lights flashing, but no siren. The city bylaw had recently put a ban on noise, and that included unnecessary use of sirens and horns.

Marlee only noticed the time when she got back to her little Mazda 3.

Shit! I'm twenty minutes late. I'd better call!

***

Spokane has six hospitals and several specialty care facilities.

Daniel was at Sacred Heart Medical Center & Children's Hospital on West 8th. They see over 71,000 emergency room patients each year. They have 30 full time physicians and dentists, and nearly six hundred RNs.

Marlee McCowan was an intern in pediatrics, who had graduated from the school of medicine at University of Washington in Seattle a year before.

So when she came in to see Daniel, she was off-duty, a private citizen. She actually didn't come to this wing at all, and knew none of the duty nurses.
"Daniel Briar, please."
"Are you family?"
"No. Is his condition serious?"
"It *is* serious. His medical bill is over $3500 and he doesn't have the money to pay it."
"We can talk about it later. Can I see him now?"

The very large nurse stomped down the hall to a ward full of outpatients, where Daniel was sitting up reading *The Spokesman-Review*, Sports Section.
"Hi! Remember me?"
"Oh hi. Yeah, of course. You ruined my week. Wanna sit down?" Daniel said.

Like most hospitals, it was crowded, and not as clean as most people would think.
Marlee sat on a stool used by med students in their rounds.

"How are you feeling? What did the doctors say?"

"Two ribs for sure are broken, collarbone too. Various scrapes and bruises. Other than that, I feel great. What happened to Ripley?"

"The convenience store owner is looking after him. Says he needs a good watchdog. You can go speak with him once you get out."

Marlee felt an urge to make contact, like she did when she hit him--but she held back.

She felt instantly attracted to this man, which made no sense whatsoever. He was a stranger, who seemed homeless, and certainly was too broke to pay his bill.

Why he would be worth five minutes of her time was a paradox that needed to be resolved.

"Well I haven't forgiven you, you know."

"Well, I kind of expected that. You have every right to blame me."

"It's not that I want someone to blame, it's that it hurts like hell and when I get out of here, I will need to be on something stronger than aspirin."

"Where will you go when you get out?"

"I haven't figured that part out yet. Rip and I are kind of homeless, so we sleep in the park. No hot showers though."

"Are you out of work? Is that why you sleep in the park?"

"I'm on a VA pension. Ex-military. I had a place back east, but had to clear out when my girlfriend showed up one night after a particularly heavy night of partying with some peckerhead, who passed out in our bed.
 I got the bus west and decided Spokane was where I would hang my hat for now."

"Look, I gotta go to work. How about I look in on you tomorrow or Thursday?"
 Marlee stood up stiffly and pulled her coat tighter.

"I'll be here," he said. "Can't be discharged until the final tests come in."
 "Goodbye, then."

Marlee stopped at the nursing station to speak with the administrator.

"I'll cover his expenses. Can I put it on my credit card?"

"Certainly, Miss. Let's wait to see what the damage is when we are ready to send him home."

"Thanks."

Marlee reached her wing in a short ten-minute jaunt from the ER. She had a lot on her mind.

***

After work most days, Marlee was running errands, shopping, and then preparing to meet her fiancé Jarrod Kennedy, a handsome local attorney.

They were waiting until after the wedding to look for a place together.

There were new housing developments starting in the valley where the price of a three-bedroom house with a large three-acre lot were well within the income bracket of both of them.

With the distant mountains as a backdrop, such a location would be the perfect place to start a new life together.

At least that was Marlee's way of thinking.

Sometimes we think that one thing is something else, or we cannot make up our minds one way or the other. Relationships are full of passages like that. Once the glow of new love wears off, reality can be cruel.

   Indecision can be excruciating, when the stakes are high. Marlee was not totally sure yet--about Jarrod. Something just wasn't jibing.
   He was ambitious in building his practice, and he could be downright aggressive when getting what he wanted. This was good for his clients, perhaps, but not so good for his adversaries in court, or those with whom he had other dealings.
   To tell the truth, he could be arrogant.
   At some level, Marlee knew that she was quite uncomfortable with him.
   He wasn't the kind of person to leave it all at work, and it did create tension between them at times. He had a temper--that was for sure. She had seen him tear a strip off a total stranger for some minor slight.

   Still, he was a catch, and at 28, Marlee knew she had to find a dependable man soon. Spokane, being a smaller city, the pool of eligibles was never that big anyway.

"*Meet me at Singleton's, babe,*" his voicemail said. That was their favorite dinner place downtown, and they did steaks well.

"Hey, Marlee. How was your day?" Jarrod ordered a Scotch and poked through the menu, although he knew it inside out.

Marlee had no intention of mentioning the incident with Daniel. It would only confuse things and upset the delicate balance needed to enjoy this evening out.

"Oh, the usual," said Marlee. " Cops brought in a young crackhead for assessment. I had to assist, as Psych is short-staffed right now. Everybody knows there is virtually no hope for these people. What a waste of a life!"

"Waste of taxpayers' money," Jarrod retorted--ordering another Scotch.

Marlee ordered the fajitas and salad, and a glass of house white. She wasn't someone who threw her money around.
She was careful with what she spent, and

careful in tracking her expenses. She had always been like that.

Now that her Dad was gone, her Mom needed her support more than ever.

And she was a birdbrain with finances. Marlee spend part of one weekend every month trying to sort out Doris' bills, tax installments--the works.

Her family had been tight, but Dad had always been the one in charge, the captain.

Lung cancer changed all that last summer, suddenly and permanently.

"You should've seen this client I had today," Jarrod said. "What an asshole! I laid out his options for suing both the insurance company and the guy who totaled his truck. He just went on like I had said nothing.

If people want to handle their own cases, why hire a $300 an hour litigation attorney? Honest to gawd, some days I think I should've been a plumber."

Marlee smiled. "You would be complaining about why people let their drainage systems or toilets back up, and swearing up and down about septic tanks."

"Yeah, you're right. It's always something. How's the wine?"

"Not too bad. It's a Chardonnay from the Okanagan Valley in British Columbia. Nice and dry and crisp. Tastes like the apples they grow up there."

"I've got to be in court all next week over this fraud case. Prosecutors are confident in getting a conviction, but that doesn't help my client, who is out of pocket at least twenty grand. We'll find out if the shadowy people behind it have any money stashed away that we can get at."

That was so Jarrod. 'Get at' the payoff, the reward. Do whatever it takes.

The other thing that was annoying for Marlee is that Jarrod never—let's say rarely—paid for her meal. He insisted on going dutch, even though he was pulling down six figures in his sixth year of practice, and she was just a psychiatric intern at a hospital with ho-hum wages.

"Once we're married, I'll cover everything, so relax." That was Jarrod's standard answer.

15

***

At this point in her internship as a pediatrician, Marlee had some decisions to make.

General practitioners were always needed in the county, but she had come to believe more and more that she could help children with psychiatric problems, and there were many.

Children were presenting in clinics and doctor's offices with a range of disorders that were uncommon in the past. Autism spectrum disorder, bipolar disorder, attention-deficit and hyperactivity disorder.

The schools couldn't keep up. They did not have the expertise or teaching resources to deal with an emerging wave of troubled kids, from kindergarten to college students.

State officials said that as many as one in four students were diagnosable, meaning mentally and emotionally— 'challenged'--was the phrase they used.

And this did not include the drug-related symptoms like low self-esteem and depression, or overdoses that were sometimes fatal.

Domestic violence was increasing in Spokane County and so law enforcement and the courts were also parties to this decline in society.

Marlee wanted to help. She had good reasons, too.

Two years ago, her younger sister Ranee had taken her life--seemingly related to undiagnosed depression related to alcohol and marijuana use that was part of the underbelly of the high school culture in America.

She was sixteen.

So now it was Marlee's chance to shift her specialty and work in a field where caring competent doctors were desperately needed.

She could maybe link up with really good medical facilities in Seattle and San Francisco for support and training. It was going to be a long process.

One of her favorites was Dr. Melvin Morse at Seattle Children's Hospital, whose extraordinary work with children who had Near-Death Experiences was groundbreaking in every sense.

That kind of thing excited Marlee.

This was her moment. A few forms to be filled in, a transcript of her medical degree, and she would be set on a new course that would give her work meaning and value.

The new internship would officially begin in October. She was ready.

Chapter Two   Bitter Medicine

Marlee began the transfer from Pediatrics General to Pediatrics Psychiatric with high hopes. She had a rare opportunity to build a practice inside of a hospital facility.

There would be no shortage of patients, and no rent or office costs to pay.
She would have prestige, and access to medical equipment no solo practitioner could possibly afford.
It was perfect. But her love life wasn't.

Jarrod was spending more time at work, or somewhere, and less time talking marriage and family.
Half the time she didn't even know where he was in town. He said he was 'busy'.

She understood 'busy'--she was crazy busy with workload and the dreaded paperwork that goes with jobs that have a heavy administrative component.

Physicians are licensed by the state and must comply with a welter of regulations, and most of it required careful—almost flawless—documentation. Patient privacy and confidentiality came close to the top of the list.

Tonight Jarrod texted he was not available, so Marlee called her buddies: Beverly, Sherrie, and Samantha. Surely one of them was free for a drink!

"What is up, my dear?" chirped Sam.

"I need a drink and I am hoping you do too," said Marlee.

"Sounds good. Bev is working tonight, but I think Sherrie is free. Lemme call her. Let's meet at The Watering Hole at, say, seven?"

"Okay," Marlee agreed. "I have something to discuss."

"Oooo, that sounds serious."

"See you at seven." Marlee removed her white coat and left it in the hall laundry for the orderlies. She brushed her hair, and studied herself in the mirror.
Maybe I should get my hair cut, she mused.

She had files to finish annotating, and if she were efficient, it could be done in time to meet the girls at the bar.

"Hey you," said Samantha, warm hugs.
"Marlee! It's been forever!" Sherrie slid into a booth and stuffed her jacket into the corner, under her purse.
"It's been a busy one," said Marlee. "I've got so much going on."
"How are the wedding plans coming along?" said Sam with a grin.

"That's just it—there's no plans, not yet. He hasn't brought it up, and I'm afraid to--you know how he is."

"Geez Marlee, you think he is right for you? I think he's a little harsh for a sweet little girl like you."
Sam was always forthright, never held back.

"Sometimes I wonder myself. It's not getting any easier to have a deep discussion with him. I hardly see him lately."

"Well, fuck a duck! Why don't you take

some time away from him and focus on your career. Am I right, Sherrie?" asked Sam.

"Men are annoying in that they do what's good for them without considering the impact on us ladies." Sherrie took a long pull at her drink.

"Haha, she should know, Marlee." Sam turned to Sherrie.
"Tell Marlee about that mechanic guy you dated last spring. What a disaster!"
"I thought he was a relatively honest dude, until I found out he was: 1) married, 2) seeing someone else at the time, and 3) not the least bit interested in doing anything but sponging off me," Sherrie said.

"But it took Bev and me three months to knock this into her head and get her to leave the prick," said Sam triumphantly.

"Shit happens," said Sherrie weakly.

"No—shit is caused!" said Samantha. "Caused by wrong decisions and a deficit of self-respect. Men wipe their feet on you like it says "Welcome". I, for one, am not a fucking doormat!"

All three friends chuckled at the analogy. It was great having buddies through all of it. They had been Marlee's for twelve years. A long time.

***

When she got home, there was a voice message on the answering machine from someone she would never have wanted to know.

"Just to let you know Marlee, Jarrod is with me, at my house. It's over, Marlee. So go fuck yourself. Don't even think about getting him back." *Beeeeeep.*

Thirty seconds of pure malice that came out of nowhere. Just like that. And it was over with Jarrod.

Marlee just sat down--too stunned to cry.

She turned down the lights, turned up the heat, and crawled under a blanket on the sofa. She just stared at the window. The moon was coming up over Idaho and Eastern Washington and cast a pale light onto the sill and hardwood floor of her apartment.

Maybe hours passed, maybe just minutes. She neither knew nor cared.

When she got up to go for a pee, she erased the vile message on her machine. *No one would ever hear those words again*, she thought. *Ever.*

It was Saturday. Marlee had slunk to her bedroom in the middle of the night and was still dopey when her cell phone chimed.

"Dr. McCowan? This is Admissions calling. We are ready to release Mr. Daniel Briar now. You mentioned that you would pay his account. Can we have a credit card number from you now?"

It was 10:30am and a bit early, if you asked Marlee.

She dug her card out of her wallet and read the card number into the phone.

"Oh-nine, 2022, yes. Thank you. Goodbye."

She hadn't even thought of Daniel lately. But she did promise to help him, to the tune of

24

nearly four thousand dollars. *Some favor*, she thought.

Where was he going to go? She wanted to know. She pulled on her jeans and top, pulled her hair into a ponytail, and dabbed some lipstick on.

It was a ten-minute drive to the hospital.

Daniel was having words with the desk clerk.

"I want to know who lost my shoes. I need my shoes."

"Mr. Briar, I can't answer that. They should have been kept with your other belongings. We can issue you a pair of hospital slippers. That's the best we can do right now."

Marlee stepped forward. "Hello, Daniel. Can I help?"

His eyes, blue as lakes, fell on her, and that feeling came over her again.

"Get me out of this circus, will you?" He put on the flimsy slippers and turned to the door.

In the car she said: "Let's go to the mall and get you some shoes."

"I wear boots, if you really want to know. And I could use some socks."

So they went shopping. Just like hundreds of families and couples on any given weekend who go to plazas and malls all over America.

For a brief moment, Marlee wondered what it would be like if it were *him*, instead of Jarrod.

"Look, Daniel, I don't have much money but how about I lend you some cash until you get settled? You can't sleep in the park the rest of your life."
"You sound like someone's mother."

Marlee blushed, but continued: "Find a room to rent, and stay there, and when you get work, pay me back if you like. Okay?"

"Why are you being so nice to me? Cause you almost killed me and my dog? I don't need anybody's sympathy, or charity. I can handle my life. *Okay?*"

His tone was mocking her words, making his point crystal clear.

"I don't mean to try to control you. Just take the money."

She wrote a check for three thousand dollars and pushed it into his hand.

"I have to go to work," she lied.

This situation was getting awkward and less than comfortable.

Daniel mumbled his thanks, and stepped out of the car.

"Hey! I don't have a number or an email for you, Marlee."

She took a business card from the glovebox and passed it out the window.

"Take care, Daniel. I promise I won't try to run you down again."

He grinned and waved.

Now why did I say that?! What a stupid thing to say.

Marlee parked and went in to make a pot of coffee and decide what to do with the rest of her life, suddenly without a partner, without someone to snuggle with, feel safe with, make love with.

***

Most of the city had evergreens—fir, spruce and pine, and this clothed the landscape in green throughout the year.

But here and there were deciduous trees that were now flaming orange and yellow as autumn advanced.

Riverfront Park was the perfect place for a stroll on such a day, and if the sun were shining, dozens of happy residents populated the attractive walkway beside the foaming, majestic Spokane River.

Small towns have gifts that big cities cannot match.

Marlee nursed a cappuccino at The Last Drop, sitting just inside out of the draft. It was packed.

Although her social life had dwindled lately, her curiosity had not.

Across the room she saw a familiar face—Daniel!

This was an opportunity to study this handsome man from afar, watch his body language, his interactions with others.

Like watching wildlife in their natural habitat.

Or maybe this wasn't his usual hangout, but she decided to just sit tight.

He put down his mug and fished in his pocket for something as he went to the payphone in the rear, near the washrooms.

She felt compelled to follow, but realized she must remain hidden.
An idea!
Marlee slipped past when he was occupied to the Ladies' room--but actually didn't go inside.
Instead she lingered out of sight, and heard him raising his voice to someone on the other end.
Is that true of all men? she wondered. *Do they all raise their voice in male bravado when they are losing control?*

"Brittney! You are out of your mind, you know that? Why would you think that?"

A couple of women squeezed past Marlee; one shot a look of amusement as she picked up on what was happening.

"There is no fucking way that's my kid!"

Daniel shot back.

There was a long pause as the person on the other end—someone named Brittney—said her piece.

Daniel just stood there, his legs stiff and his right hand propped against the wall.

"I gave you everything and this is how you thank me? Fuck you!"

Daniel slammed the handset into the cradle.

Marlee swiftly ducked into the washroom, and fixed her hair.

When it seemed time, she quietly exited, and went back to the window seat.

"Mind if I sit down?"

Daniel's sudden presence startled her, as her attention had been on the musicians out on the terrace.

"Oh. Daniel. Why yes, of course, sit. Do you need a coffee?"

"Something stronger--but sure, a double shot espresso if you don't mind. Black."

Marlee refreshed her drink and got the one Daniel requested.

"I'm surprised to see you here," Marlee admitted. "I know I shouldn't be. I mean you have every right...".

Daniel cut her off.

"Can I talk to you?" he said.

His face was tired, he had not shaved in a couple of days, and yet there was both vulnerability and anger in his expression.

"Yes. Alright." Marlee said quietly.

"I just got off the phone with my ex-girlfriend back in Buffalo. The bitch is trying to say that I made her pregnant and now she wants me to go back and support her."

"*Did* you?" Marlee was amused somehow, and decided to be catty with him.

"No. Absolutely, definitely *not*."

He sipped his coffee. "We broke up two months ago. God knows who she's been shagging since then--but not me.

What I don't get is why she is coming to me now. She knows I left the state. She knows it's over between us.

Does she think I have any interest left in her and her little tricks? She played stupid games--that is partly the reason I am messed up and on the street," Daniel said.

"I don't know if 'sorry' is the right thing to say, but 'sorry', Daniel."

"I wanted a new life, in a town where nobody knew me, make a new start," he said.

"How did she find you?" Marlee said.

"My VA checks still go to the apartment in Buffalo. I haven't got around to notifying them, partly because I did not have an address here, and they won't send to P.O. boxes."
Daniel rolled his eyes. "So I had to call her. And she dumps this bullshit on me."

"You can use my address, temporarily" said Marlee. "I know that check is important to you. We can call the Veteran's Administration office in Seattle and straighten it out."

"There you go being nice to me again. Better stop—I might get used to it," Daniel said.

Marlee's pulse picked up just a hair and she noticed it. She adjusted her hair with her fingers and sipped Cappuccino Number Two.

"I gotta go," Daniel said. "Have a lead on an apartment that I can actually afford.
And oh, by the way, the guy who has my dog—the hardware guy—offered me part-time in the warehouse down by the power station. Just having work makes me feel better. I'll keep you posted."
"Please. And get a cell phone. It's easier to reach people." Meaning herself.
"Will do. See ya Marlee!"

Marlee sat a while longer and turned over the events of the past forty-five minutes in her mind.
Is this something I really want to go forward with? Am I just being needy?
What did he mean: "I might get used to it?" Was he flirting? Or just being ironic.

Marlee picked up her purse and shawl and headed out to enjoy the rest of the weekend.
Grocery shopping, drop off skirt at the dry cleaner's, do laundry. Watch TV, eating chips.
The single life.

Chapter Three   What Are Friends For?

The life of a children's doctor was a hectic one. Children are so often sick, and when they are, it can be serious.

Strep throat, scarlet fever, mumps and measles. They are common but what is not so well known is that they are dangerous, and often cause long-term complications such as hearing loss, or impaired cardiac function.

When Marlee McCowan began the switch to psychiatry for children, she knew it would be equally demanding.

Parents were willing to accept that their little Johnny had a high fever; they were not at all willing to admit that he had 'mental problems'.

Part of the training of every psychiatrist and counselor was to recognize the guilt or shame that families feel when someone in their midst is diagnosed with a psychiatric disorder.

Denial is the first defense. It is perfectly normal. But not at all helpful.

Treatment begins with diagnosis. Here is where experience counts.

This is what Marlee needed right now.

She needed practice in assessing cognitive, genetic, developmental, behavioral symptoms.

Every psychologist and therapist uses the DSM manual, the bible of disorders of every imaginable kind.

But putting a face on bipolar disorder was challenging and had a personal emotional impact on any caring practitioner.

Furthermore, she had to consult with schools and school boards, law enforcement, juvenile courts; this added whole new levels of complexity, and, of course, paperwork.

But it had to be done. Comes with the job.

And then there was the issue of medications. Parents and patients as well often think doctors are pill-pushers, and use meds to avoid 'real' treatment.

At the end of the day, everyone—the hospital, the courts, the families—wanted to see positive results.

But results were not the same as a cure.

So many parents said: *make our kids better,*

fix them, you're a doctor!

The reality was that some kids cannot be fixed, will not respond well to treatment. They clog the jails and courts, and ruin their lives over mental problems that are largely not their fault; drug users excepted.

All the weight of the world falls on the slim shoulders of doctors like Marlee McCowan.

She wondered: *Who do the doctors go to for help in carrying all this? In doing the impossible, day by day, week by week, toiling in their clinics and labs and consulting rooms?*

***

The Monday group came after school, in order to accommodate the majority, who were students from Grades Seven to Twelve.

They were in 'group' because it was a better use of time and resources to work with patients with milder disorders and counseling issues in group therapy.

There was special training for that, and every psychiatrist learns that groups are very different scenarios than traditional office therapy.

Marlee had eleven kids in her Monday group.
A typical session would go like this:
   -icebreakers and introductions
   -round robin discussion
   -focus on possible ways to cope(for those needing it most that day)
   -wrap up.

It would run at least an hour or more. It was emotionally draining for everyone-- including the group leader—Marlee.

"Welcome, everyone." Marlee had to be upbeat and unfailingly cheerful. At 4 pm on a Monday. Have to not drink too much coffee, but enough to get you through.

"Billy? What's up with Billy today?"

Billy was bipolar—what used to be called 'Manic-Depressive'. Meaning severe mood swings. Medication was always indicated in such cases.
Today Billy was on the way down.

"I dunno. I feel bad. My Mom says if I don't take my meds, I deserve to suffer. Is that true,

Miss?"

Patients often called Marlee 'miss' instead of 'doctor'. She didn't mind since establishing emotional and social rapport was part of the process of therapy. A big part.

"No one *deserves* to suffer Billy. But your Mom is right—the medication is to help you stabilize your condition, so your life is easier to live. Right?"

Then there was Jerry.

Jerry had anger issues, rage actually. He was the son of an alcoholic abusive father who tormented his son when he was drunk; which was most of the time.

"What's going on, Jerry?" Marlee said.

"Same shit, different day," said Jerry.

"Why do you think nothing can change? Why can't tomorrow be...different?"

Marlee had to choose her words with care. She purposely avoided saying 'better' since that introduces some degree of judgment. These kids were quite allergic to being judged and were very sensitive to nuances in language.

"If I could change things, miss, don't you think I would? Soon as I turn sixteen, I'm quitting school and getting the hell out of my father's place. Thinking of the Army."

"Good, Jerry. That's very good. You need to have goals for yourself. Goals that connect you to things you enjoy doing--that others don't push in your face."
Jerry smiled. Here was a doctor who understood.
And so the hour went.
Each child a precious human being who has been damaged and who needs some kind of repair to live more or less normally in society.

Five o'clock. Day shift at the hospital is over, evening shift starting up. Nurses getting changed, administrators packing up.

EMS as well, getting ready for another night of emergency response, ready for every kind of trauma.

The heartbeat of the city, really. Police and emergency services. Keeping Spokane alive to see another day, with the sun coming up over the mountains, promising that there is a point to go on living. That there is hope.

That is what Marlee wanted to do for children—give them hope. That is what so many of them lacked. Sad.

***

Soon it was Friday. Friday was a bit easier; Marlee used it to catch up on reports and assessments. Her patient load was restricted to urgent cases only. And by appointment.

The girls wanted a night out together. Marlee was totally ready for it.

Sherrie worked east of Spokane in Coeur d'Alene, about 35 miles along I-90. If the weather was good, and the traffic not too crazy, she could do it in just over a half an hour, driving her 4x4.

Sherrie was never married, and had no kids. She put her love into her patients, since she was a nurse at the hospital there. They loved her. The administration loved her too, for her cheerful witty manner and gentle strength.

So she would be at The Watering Hole.

Sam was a legal secretary at a good law firm, and they paid her well. They had to.
She was their anchor--she knew everything about everything.

Rhonda was the only one of them who was married. She had two kids, whom she adored. She was a financial analyst at Umpqua Bank, one of the big outfits in Spokane.

And Bev--Marlee's long-time buddy since undergrad. She was a Biology and Physiology prof at Gonzaga University.
She pulled down decent money—not as much as if she had gone to Seattle, or Portland. But she loved this town—born and raised!

The whole bunch of them were tightly bound together, like a family, or a sports team with its eye on the championship. As if Life gave out trophies!

"Hey, you!" Marlee called out.

"Hey, yourself!" replied Bev.

"Huggie-hug!" The friends embraced and greeted each other warmly.

"Let's get into some serious drinking," said Samantha, ever the proactive one.

"How was your week, Marlee?" Bev asked.

"Gosh, I don't know how I'm going to do this the rest of my life. I am so exhausted!" Marlee emphasized each word, to get her feeling across.
"How was your week, Sherrie?" Marlee turned to her right.
"I'll tell you after I have two glasses of wine," she said, smiling and winking.

"Any news, Wild Women of Spokane?" said Beverly.
Bev's skill—maybe because she was a teacher—was getting the conversation going, keeping the ball in the air. And she was quite good at it.

"Marlee? We haven't heard peep from you lately. Are you that busy?"

"Last time we talked," Sam chipped in, "We

were debating the worthiness of Jarrod Kennedy to even have a place between her sheets. Am I right?"

They all chuckled, but Marlee started to cry.
"What the hell?" said Sam.
"Did something happen?" said Bev.
"Did you kick him out, like he deserved?" said Rhonda.

Marlee told them about the phone message.

"Who was she? Didn't she leave a name or number on your display?"

"No. Probably a pay phone," Marlee said.

"What do you want us to do?" said Sam. "I swear to gawd I will cut his balls off if I see him in the street."

"Amen to that," said Rhonda. Rhonda had already been through a bad marriage, and was lucky that Husband Number Two was way better.

"I have no idea," said Marlee. "I didn't see it coming. I just assumed Jarrod was working, or whatever, late every day."

"Yeah. Working on top of some little whore," said Sam.

"Oh, Marlee." Sherrie stroked her back between her shoulder blades, and Bev took her hand gently.

"Well, I'm learning to be single again," she remarked.

"Hey. Single isn't all that bad," said Sam, who was perfectly content to not have a man in her life.

Another round of drinks came.
"There is this guy..." Marlee began.

They were on her like a hawk.

"What guy?"

"His name is Daniel. I met him, ran into him—literally—on a street corner. He had to go to Sacred Heart with minor injuries. I mean he just *ran* into the street and I...I hit him."

"Why don't I understand what is going on here?" said Bev.

"So is he okay? Is he gonna sue you?" Sam was well aware of motor vehicle injury claims as her firm handled quite a few every year.

"No, but I bailed him out of the hospital, to the tune of four grand."

"Are you freaking kidding me?" Sam got to her first. "You paid his bills? And now he is eternally grateful, right? What were you thinking?"

"He has no money. He just arrived from back east, and doesn't have a penny. So I lent him so money after he got out."

"Jesus, Mary and Joseph! You need help, girl. This is because of Jarrod, that fuck." Sam was on a roll.

"It's really okay. I'm just trying to help him," said Marlee--a bit defensive now.

Beverly and Rhonda exchanged glances. Rhonda spoke first.

"This lost puppy wouldn't also be good-looking and sexy, by chance?"

Marlee was trapped.
"Well, he is kind of rugged and, yes, quite attractive in a certain way," Marlee said.

"Aha! That's it, girls!" Beverley took the lead.
"Lonely single girl runs into," she started giggling uncontrollably, "runs into a hunky guy, who gets himself hurt and needs her loving care to get better, and..."
Bev was cut off by Sam.
"...and who falls like a ton of bricks for this stranger from wherever," Sam said. "
This sounds like a stupid movie doesn't it, girls? Does he look like George Clooney or something?"

"I have a picture I took, just to have it on file, in case he disappears with the money I gave him."
Marlee tapped the screen and a photo appeared.
"Oh bullshit. You wanted something to fantasize over. Lemme see that."

Samantha leaned into Marlee to have a peek and all of them were now checking out Mr. Studly, and starting to make some rude comments about his potential as a lover.

Bev said, to everyone's surprise: "I want to sleep with him."

That got them chattering.

They realized the alcohol was hitting them now, so they ordered tons of wings and nachos, with guacamole and shredded cheddar, salsa—everything. The works.

This was a serious meeting, and required serious sustenance.

***

Daniel got things sorted out with the VA office in Seattle, which dealt with veterans all over the Northwest. They were super busy, and Daniel was lucky to get through to the person he needed.

His first check arrived at his new apartment right on the 29th. Just in time to pay the rent.

It was the letter that came a week later that really threw him.

'Dear Lt. Daniel Briar' it began.

'Upon review of your file with us, we note that your mental disability has not been reported to us as under treatment.

We require regular assessments of your disability in order to continue the benefits being paid to you.

Kindly make arrangements to be assessed, at your earliest convenience. We will give you no more than sixty days to undertake assessment and have the report sent to our office. If you need more information...'

Daniel had read enough.

Shit.

He was afraid that this might come up--he had been waiting for it. That was one reason he wanted to stay under the radar.

That, and Brittney, his stupid ex-girlfriend, who was trying to pin her pregnancy on him.

"I paid my dues, I served my country," said Daniel.

He had arranged to meet Marlee for a snack

48

and a beer after she got off work.

"Why do they want you to be assessed?"

Marlee was unfamiliar with military and defense protocols for ex-servicemen like Daniel.

"I applied for veteran benefits on the basis of having PTSD, after I served in the Middle East, and was honorably discharged."

"Post Traumatic Stress Disorder? Were you diagnosed with that?" Marlee was a bit shocked.

"That's what the Army said. The doctor said. He gave me a form I used to apply to the VA for benefits."

"How do you feel? I mean, in what ways do you experience post-traumatic stress? Is that why you were living on the street, with your dog?"

"I have trouble sleeping. Loud noises startle me. No, they upset me.
I can't control my reactions. I can get

aggressive if someone confronts me. I am...I was a soldier, Marlee.

I saw action, I saw buildings get blown up, and men get shot. It's like a nightmare that plays in my head, often when I try to sleep."

"You never said that before. My hitting you with my car must have triggered some of that feeling. My God. I am sorry, Daniel."

"Actually, no. That little accident was just what it was—a painful inconvenience. Anyhow, they will probably want me to be medicated, or have a lobotomy, or whatever it is that they do. I do not want that!"

Daniel brought his fist down hard on the table--hard enough to spill his beer.

The waitress brought a cloth and asked if he wanted another. He did.

"I have to go for an assessment, Marlee. They will put me on drugs. I will never be myself again. I can live with the nightmares and flashbacks. They are annoying but don't keep me from living my life.

What can I do, Marlee?"

Marlee ate silently, trying to think what to say to this man, this man who kept coming back into her life, into her routine, and perhaps—although she could not admit this—into her heart.

Chapter Four   Tangled

It was Bev on the phone. "Hey girlfriend, want go out?" Marlee was fine with that.

"So? Have you been in touch with, what's his name—Daniel?"
"Sort of. He's having problems with the government and has been reaching out to me."

Marlee suddenly felt protective of Daniel.
She was holding back details of what was his business, not theirs.
Or at least, honoring the confidence that it would remain private.
That is what she did with her patients. It came naturally to her now.

"Well, I could maybe do something to make him feel better. D'you think?" Bev was pushing a bit.
Marlee laughed.

Bev was a horny broad, who had not married either, preferred her independence, and not having to consult someone about where her paycheck should go. She had a pension coming in twenty years time, and she was not about to share it with anyone.

"Honestly, I don't think he's your type, Bev."

"No, but letting him get into my pants wouldn't hurt either."

Marlee tried to steer the conversation away to something else, but Bev was on a mission.

"Why not give him a call and invite him to dinner Saturday? I'll call the girls, and then we can all have a good look at him. You know, in case it starts to heat up with you two."

"He won't come," said Marlee.

"Why not?" said Bev.

"He's kind of shy I think. He's had it a bit rough lately. Break-ups and such."

"Ah! So you know more than you are letting out here, Marlee.
I think being out with four amazing women might be good for him, then.
C'mon, Marlee! You're not his auntie."

Marlee gave in. "Okay, get hold of the girls, and I will contact Daniel and see if I can convince him to swim with the sharks."

"Done!" Bev raised her glass and downed the rest of its contents.

***

There was a registered letter for Daniel at the security desk in the lobby.

Registered letters only meant one thing—legal trouble.

He opened it. It was a notice to appear in civil court.

Take note that you, Daniel Briar, are commanded to appear before the court to make response and answer to the following allegation(s):

That you, Daniel Briar, have caused one Brittney Bark, to become pregnant with child, and that she avers that the child was sired by you, on or about June 2017 and, further, that you must comply with civil and statutory provisions with respect to child and spousal support as defined by the laws of New York.

The court requires your immediate reply and attention to this matter. Failure to appear will result in judgment against you, including, but not limited to, all legal costs and fees.
 (signed)
 County Clerk for Family Court for Buffalo and Tonawanda County, New York.

A paternity suit. Brittney was serious!

"Can you believe this? I have to go back to Buffalo just to address this lawsuit, Marlee.
 I have to have an attorney, and book a flight.
 Jesus H. Christ! What did I do in Iraq that brought this bad karma down on my head?
  I was just doing my duty. I never even killed anybody. I did my stint, and I shipped back home.
 Now I'm in another war."

Marlee touched his arm, and felt the muscle and the sinews of a soldier.
 "When do you want to go?"

"You read it--the court order. ASAP. At *their* fucking convenience."

The waiter brought a beer for him, and a white wine spritzer for her.

"Then you'd better go. I'll book a flight and a hotel. This is probably a preliminary hearing to determine whether the case should go forward."

"Well, aren't *you* the lawyer today!"

"I was engaged--until recently--to a pretty aggressive criminal attorney who talked about nothing but his cases and clients--and how he was going to screw them, etc."

"I didn't know that you are engaged," Daniel said.

"I'm not. I *was*. It's over. Just forget it."

Marlee was squirming on the bench in the booth they occupied.

"Okay, not my business. I will pack my best pair of jeans and a clean shirt. Thanks a lot, Marlee. Wish me luck!"

"Good luck, Daniel. I'll contact an attorney in Buffalo that my ex knew well, and see if I can get him to represent you. Keep in touch."

Marlee put her coat on and slipped out into the cool evening wind to her car.
She didn't look back.

***

Buffalo is famous for its winters. In the snow belt--it has a foot of snow every storm that comes across the Great Lakes.
Daniel hated it. And here he was—in it.

The attorney spoke with him and notified the court that his client would appear to answer the charges. Daniel had the rest of the day to himself.

The courtroom was cool and intimidating.
The judge sits higher than everyone on 'the Bench', as it was called. Gives him or her an advantage psychologically. Civil trials rarely have juries.
Just two tables just inside the little fence they call 'the Bar'. One for Plaintiff--one for Defendant. Daniel was the defendant.

"All rise. Judge Albert Santorini presiding."

So it began. Daniel glared at Brittney, who dressed to look like a lost little sheep being stalked by a wolf. Most experienced judges know tricks like this.

"I have determined that a *prima facie* case has been made out by the Plaintiff here.
The court orders that the Defendant submit forthwith, a sample of his DNA to be tested and recorded in evidence, under seal of the Court. Any questions from counsel?"

In the hall, Daniel got to meet Brittney's new hero—Randall. He was full of piss and vinegar.

"Hey, Daniel! If you're wondering why you're here, it's because of *me*. I am doing what needs to be done—standing up for Brittney. I convinced her to get you into court. She does what I say. I say you are seriously *fucked*. See you, loser!"

Daniel lunged at him but the guard was suddenly in between, and he looked mean.

Daniel's attorney pulled him outside, and spoke quietly to settle him down.

"Look, Daniel. When they get the DNA results--and if you have been telling me the straight goods--then you will be exonerated. DNA evidence is very compelling in New York courts--trust me. Okay?

You can go back to Washington State and do what you have been doing.

There will not be a need for you to appear in court here. Normally, the attorneys work out a deal with the court, and that's the end of it."

Daniel was on the next plane to Spokane. He checked his mail, let himself in, poured himself a beer, and lay down on the couch and fell asleep.

***

When Saturday came, he found himself invited to a party, of sorts.

The girls had booked a table at Durkin's--an upscale and well-regarded bar in the downtown.

They were all dressed nicely, except Bev—she was dressed to kill.

"Daniel! How nice to meet you!" Bev made first contact. She even stroked his arm.

Talk about obvious! Marlee was thinking.

"Hello, Daniel," Rhonda said. The others followed suit.

They arranged to have him sit at the head of the table, and had pre-arranged a nice little meal with four courses, and unlimited house wine.

Yup! It was a party!

Daniel looked like a canary in a cage. He did not have a clue what to say.

Sam helped him.

"So how did you come to be in our lovely town of Spokane, Daniel?"

They engaged in small-talk like this for a while; then dinner came.

Daniel ate like it was his last meal.

He noticed that he didn't have to say much as long as he was chowing down on the rather excellent Thai-inspired chicken dish.

The food was good, better than what he was used to.

The girls were sharp. They studied him like he was under a microscope. He ignored them. Or pretended to.

Somehow, though, when the jazz band started up around nine, Bev cornered him, and leaned close, so he could see what she had to offer.

Daniel didn't have a chance. Shortly after ten, Marlee could see them leaving together-- her arm in his.

The party broke up soon after.

This would give them something to talk about next week. It really would.

Chapter Five   Kiss and Tell

Marlee had a full plate for the week ahead. New patients, a new supervisor—actually a temporary supervisor--as her regular one had gone off on maternity leave.

She found all kinds of excuses not to think of Daniel, especially Daniel going home with Beverley.

"Dr. McCowan?" A nurse was speaking.
"Could you speak with Dr. Fender in Admitting, please? We have a live one!"

"Dr. Fender? I'm Marlee McCowan from the Psych Wing. You wanted to see me?"

"Yes. Sit down. I have a newly admitted young lady who is going to need to see you after we clean her up down here. She can be considered 'high risk' and should be treated as an in-patient."

"Tell me about her."

"The patient is a fifteen year old high school

dropout who was found by her boyfriend in the bathroom of her apartment down on Second Ave. She had suffered considerable blood loss and was in shock when EMS arrived."

"He beat her?"

"No. She is apparently a cutter. She had slit her wrists--then her arms--all the way to her shoulders.
She was wearing a tank top when they found her. Some of the wounds were starting to clot. It was a mess."

"Are police going to lay charges?"

"Apparently not. This was deemed to be a suicide attempt. Now she's *our* baby."

"What's her name?" Marlee took out a notepad and started scribbling details.

"Yolanda. Yolanda Martinez.
She has no insurance, so the county is going to subsidize her until other arrangements can be made.
Oh, and by the way. There is some

suggestion that she has been selling her body. Where she hangs out is wall-to-wall prostitutes and addicts."

Marlee wrote all this down.

"Okay, Dr. Fender. Admit her and I will see her first thing tomorrow."

"Thank you, Dr. McCowan. I know she is not really a child, but you have a bit of a reputation around here as a miracle-worker."
Marlee blushed.
"No, the nurses do that part. I just listen. It's amazing how just listening to a troubled teen can help them help themselves get back on their feet."
"Well, good luck with *this* one," Dr. Fender replied.

Marlee hoped he would leave a message on voicemail, but there was nothing--no little icon to say: "Hey! Someone knows you're alive!"

She brushed and washed, and flung herself into bed. She woke up once when she snored; she only snored when she was really, really tired.

Next morning she drove to work from her apartment in Rockwood.

Rockwood was rated as the 'most livable' neighborhood in Spokane.

First of all, the median income was 57% higher than the city as a whole.

Marlee was doing well, as child psychiatrists earned, on average, $205,000 per annum, plus bonus. The median salary in Spokane was $45,000 a year.

She had a lovely two bedroom—one for sleeping, and the other was her study, full of medical textbooks and journals. Everything was tidy and in its place.

Just like Marlee.

Crime in Rockwood was 34% lower than the city overall. That was also good. She could walk at night without looking over her shoulder.

She could park underground and know that the security cameras were actually working and being monitored, and that police regularly patrolled her street, in fact, all the local streets.

It was a ten-minute drive to work from

here, which was one main reason for choosing Rockwood. Her Mom approved, and she was sure her Dad would have approved too.

Sometimes she could hear his voice in her mind.

"Don't take chances you don't have to, Marlee," or *"Trust your intuition, it's the best tool your mind has."* Dear old Dad. She missed him.

She arrived at the hospital parking; she swiped her card and parked in her designated spot.

A light dusting of early snow covered the other vehicles parked nearby. Winter was coming. No escaping it.

Marlee was not a fan of winter. She hustled inside, into the warmth.

***

"Yolanda? How old are you?"

"Fifteen." The girl lay on a cot, IV taped to her hand.

"You hurt yourself. Why?"

"I've been doing this for a while. Like when the pain gets bad."

"Tell me about the pain," Marlee said.

Yolanda said she hurt herself outside, so that the inside didn't hurt as much.

She had heard this story again and again-- history of neglect and/or abuse, no real support system, fell in with the wrong crowd.

It was like trying to straighten a pig's tail; it just went back to its twisted shape, no matter what you did.

"I have to notify your parents that you are here. You are still underage. Have you had any trouble with the law?"

Her mother came in about an hour later. She spoke softly in Spanish, and Yolanda evidently wanted to leave with her. Her mother said she would take her home.

Since Marlee could not hold her against her will, she signed the discharge form. The nurse disconnected the intravenous tube and needle, wrapped her hand, and handed her belongings over.

Just like that--Yolanda was gone--back into the darkness from whence she had come.

***

Girls' night out—it was Thursday this week--since a local cowboy bar offered free drinks to ladies.

Where the ladies were, the men would come, and flirt and frolic, with the country band rocking in the background. It was a change of scene.

Rhonda never brought her husband, of course, so she could let down her hair and just be herself.

Sherrie liked to dance.

Sam was happy just drinking beer and tapping her foot.

Bev had juicy gossip to tell.

"Where do I begin?" Beverley said, rubbing her hands together quickly, having a pull at her cocktail.

"He is very nice," she went on. "I think he was surprised to find himself in my apartment, sitting on my couch. But he warmed up to me pretty quick."

Sherrie didn't say anything, but had a twinkle in her eyes.

Sam wanted this to come out slowly, so she was low-key.

Marlee was quiet. She wasn't sure she wanted to hear any of this.

"Maybe it was just me, but I couldn't wait to pull his jeans off!" Bev was aglow with excitement, and it was contagious.
"His kisses were hard, and his lovemaking the same—but you know I like my cowboys rough--right, girls?"

The noise, the liquor, the music just amped up the mood.

"So, is this going to become a thing?" Samantha said.

"I see it coming," said Rhonda.

"Oh hell, who knows? I made him work until I got what I wanted. Three orgasms. My comfort zone."
Sexual vibes were bouncing all over the room.
Sherrie got hit on by some hunky tall guy, and was holding him close during the waltz number.
Marlee was trying to gage her feelings about Bev's adventure with Daniel.

He has a right to date who he wants, she told herself. *He doesn't deserve to be lonely.*

Sam drifted over. "You ok, Marlee?"

"Yeah, a bit tired. Long week."

"I totally get you. I have to get up at seven tomorrow, too. TGIF. Plans for the weekend?"

"Laundry... vacuum the apartment, do some mending on my favorite sweater."

"Gawd you are boring!" Sam said.

"Still getting over the shock of betrayal by you-know-who."
Marlee couldn't bring herself to say Jarrod's name. It was toxic.

"Yeah. Well if you need me, call me, for heaven's sake. I'm a phone call away."

"Thanks, Sam. I think I'm going to head out now."
Marlee hugged her buddies, and, pulling her coat tighter, stepped into the night, crystal flakes spinning around her--stars in the

streetlight.

***

Marlee decided the laundry could wait.

She punched in Daniel's cell number and waited.
"Hello," said the voice, as if Daniel didn't know who it was.
"Daniel. Can we have coffee? I need to talk to you."
"Umm, what time?"
Marlee was getting ticked off. *What do you mean—what time? You have lots of appointments today?*
"How about one? The Last Drop."

She didn't offer him a ride.

"OK, sure. See you then, Marlee."

She hung up.

The coffee place was packed--as usual. Marlee picked out a table away from the door.
Why don't they see that every time someone comes in, the cold draft hits the people sitting

there? Why don't they close the terrace door in the wintertime?

Her thoughts were tumbling like jeans in the dryer--thrashing and banging at her peace of mind.

Daniel was slightly late. Which didn't help.

"Sorry, I got delayed."

"OK. How are you?" Marlee's tone was cool, maybe even cold.

"Good. Very good. The warehouse is giving me more hours, and maybe is going to make me foreman in the Spring. *I'm* happy."

"Well I'm *not*." Marlee started in on Daniel. "You fucked my best friend!"

"No, I didn't. She fucked *me*."

There was a momentary pause, as if two combatants were suddenly aware there was a struggle in progress.

"Well that makes it a little awkward for me, don't you think?" Her voice was rising, although the ambient noise made it difficult to tell.

"Look, Marlee. I'm sorry if I did something wrong, but I personally don't think it was wrong. She just caught me at a weak moment. I fell into it."

Marlee lied.
"I don't think Bev would be too happy to hear your version of what happened."
Bev, in fact, would be thrilled to hear him complain that *she* seduced *him*.

"Why does it bother you so much, Marlee?"

"I don't know."

Marlee's indignant front collapsed.
"I'm sorry."

"Forget it," Daniel said. "How's your new job going? Too many crazies?"

She knew he was trying to mollify her, shift the mood to a more neutral one.

"Oh there's lots of work to do. I actually

didn't realize how much was involved.

I thought I could be a therapist, but I have so many reports and forms and waivers--it's nuts.

But don't get me wrong! I love it. It's just a bit much sometimes."

"I understand," Daniel said. He didn't but he said it anyway. "New Year's is coming. Any plans?"

Was Daniel fishing?

"To tell the truth, I haven't thought about it," Marlee replied.

New Year's Eve is one of those times in the year when being single can be really miserable.

Feeling sorry for yourself doesn't disguise the fact that there is a hole in your life that wasn't always there.

There used to be someone who cared for you, someone who went away for whatever reason, and now you are utterly alone.

"Well, if you are at loose ends, give me a call," Daniel said.

He sounded pitiful, Marlee thought. *Don't*

you care about my feelings?

"We can always go to The Watering Hole, or The Pourhouse. They've got live music on New Year's, I hear. Have some drinks and forget our blues."

Do you think that you can just pick me up off the ground and make me feel better somehow? Who do you think I am?

"I'll think about it. I've gotta go," Marlee said.

Daniel looked at her with his blue lakes, so deep, so attractive.

"Take care, Marlee. I mean it. You have done so much for me. I will return it somehow."

"Sure. See you, Daniel."

The conversation had not gone at all the way Marlee had hoped.

First of all, she didn't expect the upset over his night with Bev to pop out like that.

Second, she realized that her feelings were stronger than she had allowed herself to recognize.

This whole thing with Beverley brought that into the foreground. Now she had to deal with those emotions--that desire. She did not want to even think the word '*desire*', but it was there.

And it wasn't going away.

***

Christmas at her Mom's was just days away. There was shopping for food---usually turkey, and some kind of gift--that had to be done.

What to get your parents is always a headache. They always say: *"We don't need anything; save your money."* That was her Dad.

Mom said the same thing now.

What this town needs is more stores, more variety.

Marlee wished that Spokane had nicer clothing stores, a little bit better gift shops and a lot more choice in shoes. She wanted to get her Mom a decent pair of pumps. Fat chance.

The market just wasn't there for upscale shops. And she didn't have the time or the inclination to go to Seattle or San Francisco.

Wait! I'm such a dummy! I can go online and get whatever the hell I want!

So that evening, as snow sifted around the windows, she went surfing for goodies. She decided to get her an elephant made of Swarovski Crystal.

Mom had a thing for elephants for some reason. Do these peculiar preferences ever make sense, anyway?

Done! Have it ship 'Express', and it will be here by Christmas Eve. Marlee was pleased.

That left the turkey, and cranberry sauce, and stuffing bread, and all that.

She picked her Mom up, and off they went in a holiday mood.

Marlee realized how her Mom appreciated, more than ever, these —'little outings' she called them.

Red and green and gold banners and Santa posters were everywhere. There was Christmas music and favorite carols in the mall and in the stores.

You never get tired of hearing them, she

thought. *Brings back memories.*

"Let's get the turkey—while they still have any," said Doris. "Just the two of us—twelve pounds will be fine."
"Do we make our own stuffing—or get the bread crumbs and herbs one?" said Marlee.
"Let's do this the easy way this year," her Mom said.

Soon they had everything for Christmas dinner and--swinging by the wine counter--Marlee selected a Chablis to go with the turkey and dressing. It had a crisp dry flavor that was just perfectly matched their meal.

On the way out to the car she couldn't help noticing the happy couples, the women who had men who loved them, and she couldn't help thinking—just for a teeny second—about Daniel.
To tell the truth, she wanted him to come for Christmas, but how would she tell her Mom? How would she herself handle it?

Christmas and Boxing Day were just six days away, so the hospital made schedules for all the doctors, technicians, orderlies, and nurses that would stagger the workload to accommodate people's personal plans.

Marlee worked it out to be *on call only*—then she could take a much-needed break.

"I don't know about psychiatry, Mom," she began, over a glass of wine.
"It is so unbelievably intense—I'm not really sure anymore whether I can handle it.
I'm going to burn out a lot faster than I initially thought," she said.

"I was thinking about it too, dear," said Doris. "You're young—but it's going to make you old fast, I'm afraid.
Would it be any easier in Seattle, in a bigger hospital with more resources to support you?"

"I don't think it would be much different, Mom. Maybe worse.
Maybe more street kids and addicts and more red tape with Admin and Social Services," Marlee said.

"I wish your father were here," Doris said. "He was so much better than I am at figuring out what to do. He would probably say to you

'*Don't kill yourself working*' which is common sense, I guess. Know your limits, kind of...right?"

"Yeah. I haven't learned my limits yet; that's part of the problem.
I could easily overdo things and not realize it until I was up to my neck in it," said Marlee.

"I'm still sick about what Jarrod did to you," her Mom said. "He doesn't know what a wonderful girl he just tossed away."

"Well, maybe the New Year will bring someone into my life—someone I can truly trust.
Financially I'll be okay, but emotionally I'm still kind of a mess."

Marlee could not say to her mother than some of that confusion related to a guy named Daniel Briar.
And she would never mention the fact that she loaned him a bunch of cash and might never see a penny of it again.

Maybe I just have bad judgment when it comes to men, she thought.

"Okay," said Marlee. "Let's get the tree decorated! I want all my favorite ornaments on it!"

PART TWO   BY CIRCUMSTANCE

Chapter Six   New Year's Resolutions

Anyone who works in a hospital will tell you that this is a unique environment with its own unique challenges.

Ask anyone in Admitting, in Emergency, in triage—you never know who will land up on your doorstep—but you can be sure they will present with psychological issues related to whatever hurt them enough to need medical care.

This was especially true for the Psychiatry Department. Their job was to filter out the mentally disturbed population and isolate and treat them short term.

Long term, of course, it fell to family physicians and psychiatrists to manage patient treatment and care.
But hospitals took the brunt of an acute episode or the fallout from a traumatic event like a rape or kidnapping or hostage situation.

Patients could be anything from young schoolchildren--to seniors who were experiencing dementia, or abuse, or related physiological issues like diabetes or stroke.

It is a tragic reality that hospitals in every state, in every country were the front line for patient anger and pain—which they frequently took out on hospital staff— especially nurses and doctors.

More than ever, security was essential to allow staff to do their proper jobs and be safe at work.

Every day Dr. Marlee McCowan came to work was a potential crisis in the making.

It was her job description to deal with crazies and kooks of all kinds—addicts, criminals, homeless and often hopeless cases.

She had limited resources.
No long-term care beds, so not much space.
She had a range of medications including sedatives and tranquillizers.
And she worked alone for the most part.
One on one. Face to face.

A voice came over the PA system: *Doctor McCowan to Emerg...Code Green.*

Code Green. Mental patient, probably raving or misbehaving. *Call in a slim young doctor of Psychiatry and hand the case over to her. No problem.*

"Yes?" Marlee responded, sweeping into the ER from the elevator. "What have we got?"

"Kidnap victim. Young boy age nine. Was on a bus that was hijacked and taken to a hideout in the desert.
Police tracked them and recovered the bus, arrested the kidnappers—two brothers. You might get them in here later," said Judy, the Admitting Nurse on duty, with a teasing grin.

If you did not have a sense of humor you would not be able to handle the stress and tension of hospital work.

"Hello," Marlee said. "I'm the doctor. What's your name?"
"Ricky," said the boy. His manner showed he was in shock and disoriented. Typical trauma symptoms.

"You are in a hospital so you are safe now, Ricky. What can you tell me about what happened?"

She made notes of the session—as she always did, for several reasons. First of all, the hospital required detailed records of every patient encounter.

Secondly, if police and the District Attorney get involved, they will *subpoena* those records for the prosecution and trial.

Lastly, her notes were for herself. All she really had was her professional assessment leading to a diagnosis—which can be challenged in court by defense attorneys.

"Those men came onto the bus and hit the driver and threw him off. They told us we would all die if we did not do exactly what they said."

"How many of you were on the schoolbus, Ricky?"

"Most of the Fourth Grade homeroom. Maybe twenty."

"Where was your teacher?"

"They had her up at the front with them. She was scared. Most of us were crying. They said bad words to her. Those men."

"I want you to breathe deeply as you answer my questions. I am going to tap you in several places—starting with your face.
Tell me if the picture in your mind changes color or intensity as I do so.

This will help the memories fade from your mind faster; it won't hurt. I will gently tap you starting *now*."

Marlee had attended a seminar given by Dr. Roger Callaghan who had developed a unique approach to helping trauma victims using a non-invasive technique he called 'the tapping cure'.
It jibed with other techniques such as EMDR--which uses eye movements to reset the programs that anchor trauma to our memories—allowing a patient relief quickly so that the process of recovery can begin.

Ricky was sent home as an outpatient for follow-up with his family doctor.

Marlee knew that the teacher would be in worse shape if she had been assaulted or had a gun stuck in her face.
This is what soldiers and police officers often had to deal with.

'Post-traumatic stress disorder' had only recently been acknowledged as a serious and pernicious mental disorder that affected a narrow segment of the population—those who had to look Death in the face!

Marlee realized that Daniel was carrying that trauma as well.

She often wondered what she could do to help him. The basic rule of the oath that all doctors take is 'Do no harm'.

The law in the United States complemented this philosophy by requiring all doctors to get the patient's consent for each and every procedure and form of treatment.

So she would have to get Daniel to ask for her professional help and consent to whatever course of treatment she might recommend.

***

They were sitting in the coffee shop as snow came down fairly heavily outside.

It was early January and this winter was going to be a cold one, said the weather experts.

"I'm sorry, Daniel, I just couldn't do it."

"Hey, no worries. I totally get it. I upset you and you needed to get past that.

Christmas never was my favorite time, anyway. I think my unit in Iraq made a bigger deal of Christmas than my own family did," he said.

"I have been thinking about you a lot lately," Marlee began.

"It started with a patient—a kid—who was in that kidnapping incident last month.
The one with the schoolbus and the two escaped convicts?"

"Yeah, I heard about it. Why the fuck did those guys go and so something like that? They're *schoolchildren*!"

"At least one of them has symptoms of PTSD—I know, because I treated and released him."

"And you're wondering how I handle my own PTSD these days, huh?"

"I want to know more about you, Daniel," Marlee admitted.
"You strike me as someone who has held up well...I mean...you're not symptomatic...like..."

She seemed to suddenly get stuck in the middle of a thought.

"Maybe what you are saying is that you need my input on this...disorder...so you can help others who may not be as resilient—like children...am I right?"

"Right! Yeah...exactly," said Marlee. But she was just deflecting him from seeing the feelings she herself was not able to acknowledge--or was willing to.

"I never told you much about my past, I guess," said Daniel. "I don't talk about what happened overseas. Brittney didn't give a shit anyway—she only cares about herself."

The lunch he ordered came and he ate hungrily; Marlee just had a refill on her coffee.

"I got into the Air Force after high school because they made it attractive—good pay, chance to serve your country...and all that.
Plus my Dad had served in World War II and he had plenty of stories about the Philippines and fighting the Japs.
I wanted to be like him. He was a good man."

"*Was?*" said Marlee.
"Yeah, he passed away after a short illness—I think it was cancer but the doctors never really could make up their minds," he said.
"Sorry to hear that. What about your Mom?"
"She's gone too. Heart attack at 61. Too much fat from her own cooking.
Nobody made suet pies from meat like she did! A pound of fat in each meal! It was so tasty."

"Brothers? Sisters?" continued Marlee.

"I have an older sister somewhere in Oklahoma. We don't keep in touch. She's married with kids. Husband's a loser," Daniel said.

"I'm glad you have a fresh start here in Spokane, Daniel.
First of all, you survived Iraq. Second, you have enough initiative to get yourself out of Buffalo and out here to Spokane—'God's Country' we locals call it."

"Well, I had some help," he said, looking at her with a twinkle in his eye that made Marlee want to jump on his lap.

"Speaking of which," Daniel said, " I'm starting to pay you back as of next payday."

"Oh...that's not..."

"Yes it *is*," he said, and took her hand.
"This soldier pays his debts," he said. "Especially to his friends."

His face got close enough to make Marlee think he might be going to kiss her—but he didn't. Later she felt silly for having thought that.

"Can I ask you—are you taking those medications you're supposed to take?" Marlee said.

"I take 'em when I need 'em," he said defensively.

"It doesn't work like that," she said.

"Your brain has been re-wired by trauma "and needs certain chemicals to keep it functioning normally. Please, Daniel!"

Marlee realized she was being too obvious in caring about his health and well-being—to the point of nagging.

Every woman's weak point and every man's primary complaint about women.

"Okay, Doctor McCowan. If you say so.

Thanks for getting the VA to continue to pay for them, by the way. Too darned expensive for me to do it."

"It's important, Daniel. Otherwise I wouldn't say a thing to you about it."

"So...what New Year's Resolutions have you made, Marlee?" he said with a smile.

"Try and keep my balance," she said.

"Meaning...?"

"Meaning find how to handle my very demanding job at the hospital and have some kind of quality of life outside of that."

"That sounds very nice in theory, Marlee, but what does it really mean in terms of what you plan to do for the next six months?"

"I hadn't thought that far ahead, Daniel," she said. "I had plans, but my former boyfriend trashed those pretty good…"

She had to fight hard not to let Jarrod into her mind right now—let him spoil the moment.

"How about we do something together? I don't know…go skiing, hiking, plan a vacation?"
Daniel seemed to be serious now.

"Let me think about it, Daniel. It sounds good on paper," she said mockingly, "but what it works out to be with our boots on the ground is another matter."

"You are like all the smart people I ever met," he said. "You are too much in your head."

"Thanks for meeting me," she said, putting her coat and gloves on.

"So let's do it again soon, huh?" said Daniel.

This time she didn't get out of the way in time, and his soft kiss touched her lips like a snowflake. Just...barely touching.

"Call me? I got a working cellphone now," he teased, walking the other way, the snow giving way to a brief burst of sunshine on the plaza.

Marlee waved and walked to her car.

***

Bev was sipping her coffee and toying with her spoon.
"Men want sex; I want sex—he was available," she said.

"But you *knew* he was someone I was interested in," said Marlee.

"Not really. You didn't have your name on him. And from what he said the other day—you still don't," said Bev cuttingly.

"So, you are in touch with him; he didn't say," Marlee said.

"He's a single, eligible, hunky guy, Marlee. As far as I'm concerned he's fair game. Am I missing something?
I'm not thinking anything long-term but he's just fine in bed and that's all I want right now."

"Sure," Marlee said. "Go for it. I don't want to get in your way. I'm glad for you, Bev. You deserve to be happy."

Marlee was feeling numb like someone had punched her. Only it was her BFF--and it hurt even more.
She wanted to yell at Daniel—tell him he was a lazy-ass and a liar. Something.
She wanted an excuse to confront him.

Deep in her heart she just wanted to see him, be close to him.

She really wanted to scream at him: 'I found you *first*...you *owe* me!!'

"Gotta go... I'll call you," said Marlee grabbing her purse.

"Marlee, I'm sorry," Bev started to say, but Marlee just snapped: "Forget it" and was gone.

***

When Marlee called Sam, Sam knew right away something was wrong.

Sherrie came in to town and Rhonda was there, too. Bev had not been invited, Sam said.

"So Bev has done an end run around whatever you've got going with Daniel," Sam said.
It was a question but she said it like a statement of doom.

"I've got to talk about this," said Marlee. "You guys are my team. I admit I'm really bent out of shape by this. I should have realized that I'm not the only game in town.
It's just that I saved him, I've been his best friend and...it's not *fair!*"

To everyone's surprise, Marlee burst into tears--which was not her style.

"Well, crap," said Samantha. "If this were anyone other than Bev..."

"Maybe we should take Bev aside and talk to her, explain how much it is hurting Marlee," said Sherrie.

Marlee was dabbing her eyes, saying: "No!"

"I can fight my own battles thank you. I will figure something out. I just wanted to vent."

"Has anybody asked Daniel what *he* wants?" asked Rhonda, trying to sound hopeful.

"Well, he seems content to bang Bev and ignore Marlee for the moment," said Sam.

"Have you talked to him?" asked Sherrie.

"We had coffee recently," replied Marlee. "He told me he'd got an apartment and was getting paid decent money at his new job."

"Did he say something? I mean, about...you? Or Bev?" Sherrie continued.

"No. *I* did most of the talking, I think.
 I wanted to tell him why I didn't invite him home for Christmas—but when the time came, I fizzled out.
 Just couldn't put it together to tell him I was struggling--with everything."

Now Rhonda waded in.

"Just a freakin' minute here, ladies. This is a guy who was homeless and presumably broke who Marlee picked up off the street..."

"...after running him down!" quipped Sherrie.

"After hitting him with her car," continued Rhonda, " ...and gave him nothing but kindness..."

Sam cut her off.

"...and *cash* and paid his hospital tab!"

"Yeah," said Rhonda.

"And this is how he shows his gratitude? Hopping in the sack with Marlee's best friend? Give me a fucking break!"

Rhonda was all but shouting now.

"We need more drinks," said Sam— ordering another bottle of white and some finger food.

"So—what are you saying?" said Sherrie.

"This guy is not worth the hassle? Push comes to shove—I agree.

Marlee! You deserve the best man in town! I hate to say it but your luck has been shit lately.

Jarrod...now Daniel...we need to find you a *real* man!" Sherrie said.

"Something to think about, Marlee," said Sam, pouring everybody a glass.

"Here's to finding Marlee a good man!" and Sam and the girls raised and clinked their glasses noisily.

My friends are right, Marlee was thinking on the drive home.

Is Daniel just playing me? Am I just a sucker to think we might have a chance?

Why did he kiss me? Or say those things?

If he is sleeping with Bev, why did he say those things to me about holidays and plans?

Marlee threw herself into bed and turned the lights off.

Chapter Seven Ups and Downs

"Well I can play tit-for-tat," said Beverly.

"I'm sorry I said anything!" said Rhonda dolefully.

"She's just upset, Bev," added Sherrie. "I mean—wouldn't *you* be?"

"Well, something is going on—I haven't seen Daniel and he hasn't called me, so what am I supposed to think?" said Beverly.

"I just don't see Marlee playing games, and she didn't say one word against you, Bev," said Rhonda.

Sam bustled in and slammed herself down into a seat.

"Spritzer!" she hollered to the waitress.
"I can tell from your faces that we are still on the Daniel thing," she said.

"Look! Let's not make this an issue, girls!
Both Bev and Marlee are interested in this guy but he's not worth getting bent out of shape about!"

"I agree," Bev said. "Maybe he's just a typical man who expects favors but offers very little in return."

"I'll drink to that!" Sam and Rhonda said together. "Cheers!"

***

Marlee got a text from Daniel.
I need to ask you a favor. Can we meet?

Marlee had gotten off early since her Monday group had been cancelled this week.

She was nursing a glass of red when Daniel came in and slumped into a chair across the table from her.

"You look discouraged," Marlee said.

"Yeah. Haven't heard anything from the lawyer about the paternity suit in Buffalo. That usually means things are not going well.

It's taking too long.

And to make matters worse, I got laid off for a bit. The warehouse is having financial issues and they are cutting back.

The good news? I've got on with the State Forestry Department as a firefighter.

They are predicting a bad year for forest fires since we didn't get enough rainfall or snowpack in the mountains and the woods are already dry as tinder."

"Forest fires?" said Marlee with surprise.
"That means you will have to go out of town doesn't it? Out into the boonies?"

"Yes, yes it does. But I'll be making decent money and live-rent free in a fire camp with free food and all the fresh air I can handle!"

His voice betrayed a small ripple of excitement, as if he had been clever to pull this temporary job off.

"So...we won't see you for a while, I guess."

Marlee's voice trailed off although she didn't realize it.

"Yeah, I guess so. Ah, Marlee—I need to ask a favor."
"That's what your text said. What do you need? Money?"
"I wish you wouldn't say that—like I come to you for money all the time," Daniel said hotly.
"No-I mean..." Marlee shrank back in her seat.

101

"It's Ripley. Remember my dog?"

Marlee nodded and nervously tipped the last of the wine down her throat.

"I can't take him. I don't want to leave him with that store owner again, and I don't have anyone other than you I can ask."

His gaze was direct and earnest and Marlee felt a quiver in her tailbone.

"Oh, sure, no problem, Daniel," she said without thinking.

"He needs to be walked twice a day but other than that, he won't give you any trouble.
I will pay for his food—he eats about as much as I do!" Daniel said with a laugh.

"He won't expect to sleep on the furniture will he? He won't jump on me in the night or something?" said Marlee.

"No. I'll bring his blanket and he can sleep in the kitchen or hall—whatever works for you.
He's a good watchdog. You might get used to having him guard you at night," Daniel said hopefully.

"When does all this take place?" inquired Marlee.

"Next weekend," he said. "The Forestry crew will swing by my place early and we head west into the Cascades."

"What about your apartment?" Marlee asked.

"A student from Gonzaga is going to sublet it for the time being," he said. "She's a neat freak so I know she won't trash the place."

"When shall I come for Rip?" she said.

"How about Thursday? Does that work for you?
We could grab a bite then you drive me home and we'll load Rip into the back.
Your Mazda is a hatchback, right?"

"Yes, it's very convenient for loading groceries...and homeless dogs!" This time she was smiling.

"I will miss you," said Daniel.

"You will be busy trying to stay out of harm's way," she replied.

"I can't imagine standing in a forest on fire—how do you know you will even get out?!"

"Well, the forestry guys have it all worked out," he said. "They deploy squads of men to various tasks such as digging trenches and falling trees to create a firebreak, to walking right into the blaze and smoke to hose down the fire or prevent it from climbing.

Once it gets up into the treetops and there's a wind, that so-called 'crownfire' will spread very fast and that's what we don't want to see happen."

"Well keep me posted, Sergeant Briar!"

"How did you know I was an NCO in the service?" he asked.

"I saw your VA benefits statement, remember?"

"Oh, right. You know everything about me, Marlee," he said.

"Not just yet," she replied. "Call you Thursday."

Daniel held her for a moment--murmuring his thanks. It was a longer moment than it should have been.

What is that look in his eyes saying?
Marlee wished she could read his mind.

She went home and vacuumed.

Then she realized it was silly to clean the house when your only guest would be a sixty-pound boxer who would track in mud and god-knows-what.
Well at least he wouldn't shed.

***

When Thursday came, Daniel was in a happy mood.

Mizuna's Restaurant & Wine Bar was very well-regarded in Spokane and they took a corner booth in the tastefully planned out space on North Howard Street.

They had good wine—not just local—but French and Australian wines with some vintage. The menu was excellent and both of them started to relax with a glass of Shiraz from Down Under.

"I have the *best* news, Marlee!" Daniel started.

He pulled a letter from his jacket pocket and handed it to her.

"The DNA tests prove I am NOT the father, and Brittney is full of shit. It's not my problem anymore. I'm a free man!"

Marlee read the lawyer's letter addressed to Daniel and outlining the reasons for the judge's decision to acquit Daniel Briar.

"That's fantastic!" said Marlee--clinking her glass against his.

"It feels like ten tons lifted off my back," said Daniel. "It means I never have to go back to Buffalo--ever!"

"So you have decided to make the Lilac City your permanent home?" teased Marlee.

"That's the plan!" he said enthusiastically.

"Good plan!" said Marlee leaning over the table to put an arm around his neck and pressing her lips against his cheek.

She drove him to his apartment and they loaded the dog into the car.

"I don't know when I will see you next," he said awkwardly. "Take care, Marlee."

Once more she embraced him—as if they were already close...lovers? friends?
"You'd better e-mail me or text me or whatever, Daniel. I want a regular report from you so I know you are okay out there. Okay?"

"Yes, ma'am," he said dutifully.

He stood in the road without waving—but watching her car recede into the distance.

***

Ripley was an easy dog to get along with.
Feed him, walk him—and not much else.
He was well-trained Marlee realized.

Too bad men aren't the same, Sam would have said.
Marlee was enjoying having a watchdog on the premises.

Maybe it was her imagination, but she slept better and had someone to talk to—so to speak.
It wasn't like being a mother, she reflected. But it brought out her caregiver instincts all the same.

She wanted to have dinner with her mother and called to arrange it.

"Hello, sweetheart, I thought you'd forgotten me," Doris said.

"Has it been that long?" Marlee replied.

"Christmas was seven weeks ago, dear. I've taken down the ornaments and tossed the tree ages ago."
"I'm sorry, Mom. Can we have dinner this week? I'll cook--but at your house. Pasta okay with you?"

"Whatever you like, darling. I liked the way you did the shrimps and mussel sauce.
 They've got fresh seafood in at Manny's Market if you'd care to swing by there on the way. How's Friday?" Doris asked.

"Good," said Marlee. "I'll get a baguette and a bottle of Chablis as well. See you then, Mom," she said and hung up the phone.

Both Marlee and her Mom had landlines because they were reminders of the times past when life was somehow simpler, when her Dad was around to tinker with his tools and get under Mom's feet.

She missed him.

She regretted that he couldn't be here to see her building her medical career at the hospital—the same one that he died in, in the ward where terminal patients stay until their time comes.

Just then the phone rang.

"Hello?" she said.
"Marlee—it's me," Daniel said.
"Daniel? Where are you?"
"About a million miles from where you are," he said.

"I'm in a small town that I don't know the name of—except it has a tavern that is welcoming to firefighters and forestry guys and the beer is cold."

"Are you okay? Is there a fire you're on?"

"Funny you should say that," he replied.

"We spend three days getting equipment and supplies into camp, and then had nothing to do—so we took the four-by-four into town.

We got a call over the radio that a fire had just gotten started about twenty miles up the mountain.

So tomorrow we ship out and go to check it out.

I just called because...I miss Rip—how's he doing? Not being a nuisance I hope?"

"Not in the least. He and I have an understanding..." she put the receiver to the dog's ear.

"Say 'hello', Daniel."

"Howdy pardner!" said Daniel, and the dog's ears pricked up right away and Rip gave a low woof—as if Daniel were hiding in the corner or something.

"We miss you too," said Marlee. "Don't go falling in love with any small-town bar girls, huh?"

Daniel laughed.

"They're all married and over forty," he said.

"Thanks for the call, Daniel. Look out for yourself."

"Sure. I will text you when I get off this fire. Might be a few days, though."

"Sure. Say 'goodbye' to daddy, Rip!"

The line went dead and Marlee went to the cupboard to get the kibble that Rip liked to eat.

Oddly, the phone rang again.

When Marlee answered she found it was Bev on the other end.

"Hey. Do you want to meet for coffee? I've got something I want to discuss with you," said Beverley.

Marlee felt her heart sink.

"Ah, sure? Like—alone? Or with the girls?"

"At this point, I don't really care. If you can get them to come, we can meet at The Watering Hole.
Otherwise, there's that coffee place Mrs. Bean near where I work that is a bit private."

"Let's do it that way," said Marlee. "I'll meet you there about eleven-thirty in the morning."

"See ya," said Bev.

Now what? Marlee was asking herself.
I do not want a fight, I do not want bad feelings here.
What am I going to say?
I don't even know what I want out of this Daniel business.
If only I hadn't hit him with my car...

***

Mrs. Bean was where you went to get unusual blends—like Ethiopian and Kenyan or Brazilian and Costa Rican coffees.

Their barista was a trained sommelier that specialized in exotic coffee and tea.

Marlee waited with her macchiato for Bev to arrive.

"Sorry," said Bev—out of breath—"I had a last minute thingy with my boss."

"I ordered the same thing for you that I got for myself," said Marlee. "Then we can compare and make comments about it."

"I won't mince my words here, Marlee." Beverley seemed red in the face but maybe it was the sunlight reflecting off the awnings.

"I have not heard boo from Daniel, and I'm a little bit steamed about that. Did you say something to him?"

"No."

"Can you think of a reason why he would avoid me, then?" Bev went on.

"All I know is he got laid off and joined the Forest Service fire crew and buggered off to someplace in the Cascades near Mt. Rainier," Marlee said.

"How do you know *that*?" said Bev accusingly.

"He told me," replied Marlee. "He left last Friday."

"Excuse me—but why would he tell *you*—and not me?"

"Cause he needed me to look after his dog," said Marlee, matter-of-factly.

"You've been keeping him at your house behind my back—is that the case?"

"Look, Bev. He's not my boyfriend, he's not been anywhere near my apartment—let alone my bed—and I really don't know how you got the idea that I was somehow keeping him from seeing you.
 I have zero interest in that—even if I were somehow interested in the guy—which I am *not*."

Marlee told a fib. But at the moment it seemed the best course of action.

Anyhow, what she said was substantially true—he wasn't her lover or anything like it.

"So then he just rode out of town like some goddamn cowboy on his high horse."

Bev meant it to be a question but it came out flat—like a done deal.

"I'm sorry, Bev," said Marlee suddenly. "The very last thing I wanted was for this to come between us."

To Marlee's surprise Beverley started to cry and dab tissues at her eyes.

"I think I put more of myself on the line than I wanted to," she said between sobs.

"I think I fell for this guy before I even knew anything about him. I feel like such a fool."

Marlee wanted to reply to that, wanted to admit that she, too, had been a fool for Daniel.
But she just couldn't let it out—not now and not here. Not yet.
There were many loose ends.

Marlee stroked Bev's arm affectionately.

"You know what? Let's just put him right out of the picture, Bev.

Let's get back to *us* and the fun things we share and do together.

Let's go to see a mindless movie like *The Madman of Paris* with...with...oh what the heck is his name? Dépardieu?"

Bev dried her nose once last time and started to smile—that's when Marlee knew it would be okay between the two of them.

Bev went back to work and Marlee headed for the hospital. Little did she know that a bomb cyclone of the legal kind was sitting on her desk.

***

It was a summons to appear—a subpoena—to give testimony in the trial of a former patient who had been arrested for assault with a weapon.

It was short on details, as these legal documents often are, but the court wanted to see Marlee--and her notes--to give testimony as to the mental fitness of the accused.

She had to be on call in fifteen minutes—which didn't leave a lot of time to paw through her casefiles under 'F'.

Farber...Fenster...Filipchik...here it is.

Josep Filipchik, age 37, employed part-time as a janitor at a local community college.

Diagnosis: paranoid schizophrenic prone to violence when under severe stressful conditions.

Treatment of choice: chlorpromazine, oral, twice daily--combined with talk therapy weekly until symptoms are well-controlled.

Treatment notes: started on drug at low dose with gradual increase to 40mg daily.
Patient symptoms subsiding—particularly hallucinations and delusionary episodes.

Rational-Emotive Therapy shows promising results in initial treatment plan.

Patient released from long-term care into custody of his wife, as of 11/03/19.

Patient requested by e-mail to remain in regular communication with supervising physician.

Marlee had no time right now to speculate on what went wrong with Mr. Filipchik that landed him in jail.

She was required in the ER for a bipolar case that was in the manic phase for a disturbed young woman.

When she arrived, Security had restrained her and were looking plaintively at Dr. McCowan as she swept in the door.

"Sixty milligrams benzodiazepine," she barked at the intake nurse.
"Injectable. Make sure it is in the muscle not the vein."
All the while Marlee was trying to calm the patient and reassure her that she was not in any kind of danger.

The drug worked quickly and she was taken on a gurney to Psych to be monitored.

The nurse said she could not handle the out-of-control patient—that's why she called Security.

"You're new here," commented Marlee.

"Yes," the nurse said--who appeared to be about nineteen.
"You'll get used to it," said Marlee. "Never a dull moment around here!"

She smiled and couldn't resist asking: "How old are you?"
"Twenty-three," she replied.

"Wow! I'm Dr. McCowan, by the way."

"Lily Wang. Nice to meet you!"

"We're seeing more opioid cases—in fact a lot of drug overdoses in general," said Marlee.

"Methamphetamine is a big problem among young people, street people," she went on.

"Drunks don't normally show up at our door and anyway they are more annoying than dangerous. But druggies? Look out!"

Nurse Wang looked petrified, so Marlee offered to get her a coffee but she produced her little gold thermos with green tea and even offered Marlee a cup.

"Oh! It's tasty," said Marlee.

"Has a caffeine hit equal to any cup of coffee though," Lily teased. "This one is called *pu-er cha*," said the nurse. "It one of China's best teas!"

"Thank you, Lily! I think I'm going to become a believer in green tea.
My pager just went off so I'd better go check on that girl in Psychiatry. See you later!"

"See you, Dr. McCowan," said Lily.

"Oh call me *Marlee*," Marlee said.

"It's weird for me to call someone in authority by their first name," Lily replied. "We never do that in Chinese culture. It would show disrespect."

"I see," said Marlee. "I like that. Bye for now."

   ***

Jarrod would know what to do with this legal business, she mused. *He's a criminal lawyer and deals with this every day.*
Just when I need the guy...

Marlee reflected on the irony. *Jarrod was probably married now—to someone else.*

The trial date was next Wednesday so she made arrangements to book off the morning.

She got home after dark as it was still April and daylight savings had just kicked in.

Ripley was all face-licking and tail-wagging as she put him on his leash for his walk.
At least somebody is glad to see me.

The park at this time of day was full of dog-owners and she stopped to acknowledge some of the people who lived in her building.

Dinner tonight would be something that goes in the microwave, she decided.
Just can't gather the energy to cook and too lazy to go out and eat alone somewhere.

She switched on Netflix and dug her fork into the lasagna—not too bad if you get the pre-cooked meat lasagna.
Rip curled up right on her feet; maybe he felt the loneliness just like she did.

***

She put on a two-piece suit that was navy blue, with matching pumps, and gold studs for earrings that were modest but tasteful.

The courtroom was a bit more crowded than she expected. There was a media guy there with his camera crew.
She heard someone in the gallery whisper: "Psycho slasher!" to his friend sitting next to him.
So! That's why the fascination, and why the TV crew!
Everybody loves a drama—take a criminal who is mentally disturbed and the whole world wants to be in on it.

"All rise," said the officer-at-arms.

The judge came in and sat down up there on his 'bench'; the accused was in a plexiglass 'prisoner' box'.
The District Attorney was shuffling papers—so it wasn't until the last minute that she got a glimpse of the defense lawyer.

She wanted to faint.
It was Jarrod!

The DA rose and began reading the charge and laying out the evidence: the police report, and crime scene, the witnesses—even the victim's statement.

Oh thank God it's not a murder trial!

Marlee was thinking she was like a deer in some truck's headlights—never been in court as a witness before and clueless as to what might happen.

The Defense had pleaded *'Not Guilty'* at the outset and now Jarrod stood up and addressed the judge.

There was no jury since the accused can choose trial by judge alone—which simplifies things a lot for both sides.

It also costs the taxpayers a hell of a lot less money.

"Your Honor, I would like to point out to the court that the accused has a serious mental disorder and has been in psychiatric care for over two-and-a-half months."

The audience was loving it. A real-life psycho sitting right there!

"It is our position that the accused—Josep Filipchik—an honest, hardworking immigrant should be held 'Not Responsible' for his actions due to his unstable mental condition.
In fact, we would argue that there was no intention to harm anyone—that he was reacting to a perceived threat to his person.

What I am saying, your Honor, is that he acted in self-defense."

The crowd murmured and heads turned and the judge had to bang his gavel and shout: "Quieten down. Order in the court!"

They did. It was so quiet you could hear a paperclip drop.

He sat down with that smirk on his face that Marlee knew so well.

Jarrod liked to win and was used to having his way with the judge.
He was one of the core members of the state Criminal Bar Association.

The DA stood up, turned, and said: "I would like to call Dr. Marlee McCowan to the witness stand."

Marlee's heart dropped right into her shoes.

The little gate opened and she walked unsteadily to where she was to give testimony.

"Do you swear to tell the truth—the whole truth—and nothing but the *truth*, so help you God?"
Marlee's slender hand rested on the maroon cover of the Bible and said: "I do."

"You may sit down," said the officer.

Vague whispers could be heard from the public gallery—running like a fire through the treetops.

"You have treated the accused in your practice at Sacred Heart Medical Center, is that correct?"

Marlee looked at the DA and tried to avoid Jarrod's hawk-eyes.

"Yes, sir."

"Were you the doctor who diagnosed the accused with schizophrenia?"

"Yes, sir."

"Would you tell the court, Dr. McCowan, a bit about schizophrenia and its effects on someone who has this disorder?"

Marlee patiently--and in as loud a voice as she could muster—told the court about this serious disease: the hallucinations, and bizarre behavior, the distorted thinking.

Jarrod was grinning.

Marlee realized she was just playing into his hands.

He was going to say her testimony proved his point—that Josep Filipchik is too crazy to have known he was assaulting someone with an iron bar and should be found 'not guilty by reason of insanity'.

All this ran through her head as she was finishing answering the DA's questions.

But the DA had a plan, too.

"What is the standard treatment for a psychotic patient, Dr. McCowan," he said.

"The treatment of choice is—and must be—strong anti-psychotic medication, which I prescribed for him.
This allows the patient to gain control over the overt symptoms.

Then psychotherapy involving cognitive psychology is used to complement the drugs.

The idea is to help the individual resume a normal existence and to function in society again."

Now it was Jarrod's turn--on cross-examination.

"Dr. McCowan, are you certain that you prescribed the *right* medication for this individual?"
His evil eyes bored right into her.

"I followed standard protocols in psychiatry," she said.

"What would be the effect of giving the *wrong* medication, or the *wrong* dosage of the right medication, Doctor?"

"There would be a poor prognosis for the patient and he or she would need to be admitted and re-assessed," Marlee said.

She was keeping her cool.

She told herself that this cheating son-of-a-bitch was not going to push her around--here, or anywhere!

"So isn't it the physician's responsibility to check up on the patient from time to time? To see how they are coping?"

"I send e-mails to patients and their caregivers to remind them to come into the hospital and be examined, and for therapy which is complementary to the medication," Marlee explained.

"What if the patient doesn't get the notification? What if the patient is in distress and cannot function well enough to respond?"

"That is outside the scope of my professional responsibility, sir," said Marlee with an edge in her voice.

"*Is* it?" said Jarrod accusingly.

"Objection, your Honor," said the DA.

"Counsel is badgering the witness, and his line of questioning will produce no useful information whatsoever."

"Objection sustained," intoned the judge.

"No further questions, your Honor," said Jarrod, slamming himself into his chair.

Marlee needed a coffee. As if hearing her, the judge called for a short recess.

Marlee exited through the gate and headed to the Starbucks just outside the courthouse.

She had one message from her mother to remember dinner on Thursday this week.

She downed the coffee and headed back into the lion's den.

When they put the accused on the stand, at first he said he didn't remember anything about the incident.

When pushed by the DA, he said he was attacked outside the bar in the parking lot by the Devil himself.
He didn't remember striking this individual.

"You don't remember picking up an iron bar and hitting him?" asked the DA.

"Not really," said the witness evasively.

"Then how did you expect to get in your car and drive home if you were so out of touch with reality?"

"And if you were having a psychotic episode, what were you doing drinking in a bar in the first place?"
The DA was relentless.

"If you were attacked by The Devil—what did he say to you? What did you say to *him*?"

"I just remember his evil laughter and he smelled like sulfur—like Hell itself!" said Josef.

"You called out for help, is that correct?"

"I shouted and two men nearby came to help," he said.

"How did you know *that*--if you were having hallucinations?
You can't have hallucinations one minute-- and call for help and be aware that others were helping you--the next!"

"Let me ask you one question, Mr. Filipchik.

Were you taking your medications regularly? Do you remember taking your pill that morning?"

The accused then dropped a bombshell.
"I lost them; I lost the bottle of pills the doctors gave me."

A ripple in the courtroom.

"So what you are saying is that the night you encountered The Devil—you had not been taking your pills at all. Is that correct?"

"I told you—I lost them. I couldn't find them."

The accused was becoming more and more agitated with the questioning from the DA.

The judge noticed it, Jarrod noticed it, and Marlee noticed it.

"Your Honor, I submit to you that the accused *should* be held responsible for his actions insofar as he has been *negligent* in taking the medications he is supposed to be taking--and can't hide behind his disease to avoid liability in this case."

The DA continued standing after speaking.

Before Jarrod could reply, the poor man in the witness stand started wailing and pulling at his hair.

For a moment no one had a clue what to do.

Filipchik shouted: "Kill! I will kill!"

The judge waved at Marlee and said: "Doctor? Can you do something?"

Marlee was ushered into open court and approached the anguished man.

"Josef?" she spoke in a soothing tone.
"I'm going to give you some medicine now to help you feel better, okay?"

She tore open the paper wrapping on the syringe and plunged it into a small vial with a silver foil cap.
She fumbled with his sleeve but got the shirt up far enough to expose his triceps muscle in his upper arm—then drove the needle home.

For reasons she could not explain, her intuition had suggested to her to take a powerful sedative—diazepam—in her purse today.

Call it 'doctor's instinct'.

But it immediately worked to settle the witness and allow the guard to lead him out of the courtroom—into safe custody.

For which the judge thanked Marlee profusely.

The DA did as well and said she would not be required to attend the afternoon session where the lawyers would haggle about what kind of sentence was appropriate.

Marlee agreed to fax a new prescription of Josep's anti-psychotic drug to the court clerk so he could be stabilized in his cell--awaiting sentencing.

The last thing Marlee remembered was Jarrod looking at her—humble now, for a change.
She thought he might have had a look of actual respect—although with Jarrod it was hard to tell.

Chapter Eight   Danger Ahead!

She breezed into her mother Doris' kitchen with the groceries.

"What a week, Mom! You wouldn't believe!"

"Pour yourself a glass of wine, dear and just unwind a bit before we start cooking."

She told her mother about the courtroom drama and Jarrod's insufferable arrogance.

"Well, you escaped his clutches and *that's* good news!" her mother said.

"I don't get paid to do this," she said—meaning getting grilled in a court of law!

"True," said Doris. "You deal with enough nonsense at work, dear!"

They clinked glasses and sat back on the sofa.

The sun was sinking in an orange glow behind the distant Cascades; for a moment Marlee thought about Daniel in those mountains.

Was he all right? Was he battling a deadly fire today?

"Mom—turn on the news will you?"

The announcer was showing video of an enormous forest fire burning a thousand acres of prime timberland east of Mt. Adams.

Daniel had to be there somewhere!

Then the news switched to a Seattle story about a girl who tried to feed a seal from the dock and it grabbed her jacket and pulled her in right off the dock.

She was okay, but both tourists and locals were shocked, and there was endless chatter about seal behavior and why kids need to be taught to respect wildlife in its natural environment, and...blah-blah-blah.

Marlee switched off the TV and started the pasta.
"Shall I peel the shrimp?" said Doris.

"Let's do it the Chinese way and leave them cook in their shell. We can peel them when we serve and eat," said Marlee.

The whole house began to smell like seafood and it was very appealing to both of them.

"Oh, by the way, a postcard arrived, dear. I forgot to tell you. It's on the mantle."

Doris took the card showing the vast green carpet of trees typical in the coastal region of the Pacific Northwest on one side, and a scrawled short message on the other.
It was from Daniel.

"Why did he sent it *here*," Marlee inquired.

"Maybe it's the only address he has for you, dear. Does he know you have your own place?"

"Of course, Mom," said Marlee. "He's never been to my place; but he's never been here either.
Why would he mail it *here?*"
She was thinking out loud.

"Well—read it, dear. What's the date on it?"

"Last week. It must have been when he just got settled in the fire camp," said Marlee.

"Oh he was homesick!" said Doris.

Miss you a lot. I look up at the stars and I feel how lonely they must be in the infinite space that separates them. Wish you were here, Daniel.

"I think you are right, Mom."

"I think he must have feelings for you, Marlee," Doris continued.

"Maybe. He called me last week and asked how Ripley was doing. I know the call wasn't just about his dog. Men are so needy."

"That's why they have a wife, dear," said Doris.
Marlee changed the topic.

"What do you want for your birthday coming up, Mom?"

"Surprise me!" Doris replied.

"Hmmm...okay. I'll think of something."

    ***

Marlee decided to keep an eye on the wildfires burning in Washington State with a bit more attention.
The last few years had seen a significant increase in fires on the West Coast.

Some areas—like British Columbia—had had record burns that even threatened some of the important towns in the Interior.

California had seen a frightening fire burn a little town called Paradise to the ground. A fire so hot that it melted a car!

Global climate change was kicking in as the new normal—and storms with ferocious winds and rain or hail were frequent right across America.
Forests were threatened like never before and yet governments—especially the Feds—were slow to respond with needed resources to put men on the ground.

Daniel's crew was a response to the state of emergency that was a product of global temperature rise—our planet was burning right before our eyes!

This summer was predicted to be as bad. Nobody in government or media wanted to state the grim possibility that it might even be *worse.*

This is KING-TV and it is six o'clock on the West Coast. Here is the news.
A massive wildfire burning east of Mt. Adams has only been 18% contained and thousands of acres of timber are threatened as winds have picked up.
Our reporter, Lisa Yann is on the ground near Snoqualmie. What can you tell us, Lisa?

And so the broadcast continued with scary pictures of smoke and helicopters dropping water and dirty men trudging in and out of the bush in the watershed that provides Seattle-Tacoma its drinking water.

There are reports of casualties among the residents and firefighters as they fight a losing battle...

Marlee's ears pricked up. *Casualties? Like--people are dying?*
This was out of her hands, she thought.
Natural disasters happen—and all communities can do is to react and try to recover.

Anyhow, Daniel is ex-military and knows how to handle himself in danger, she told herself.

She got ready for bed as she reminded herself that she had a heavy caseload this week. Crazy people were coming out of the woodwork.
Maybe it was the change from winter to spring, maybe it was solar storms that blasted rays of powerful energy at Planet Earth from time to time.
She set the alarm and turned off the bedside lamp.

***

The new nurse Lily Wang greeted her.
The head nurse coming off night shift did too.
"Nothing to report, Dr. McCowan," she said. "Nothing that can't wait, anyway. See you tonight!"

Marlee unlocked her office door and threw her purse on a chair. She slipped out of her coat and hung it on the back of the door.

That is when she noticed the note.

It had been slipped under the door sometime in the night, she guessed, and picked it up and read it.

Im watching you. Im coming for you. Are you reddy for me, doctor?

No punctuation, no signature. Misspelled word.

Oh God...it's a patient... Marlee deduced.

But who?
Someone who knew where her office was, knew she was female and was going to be alone and vulnerable at times.

Josep Filipchik was in jail. So...not him.

Marlee ran through her mind to see if any red flags popped up as she mentally scanned her list of patients who would be scary enough to threaten her in this way.

Warren? Randy? That nutcase who called himself Judas?
Judas was Jerry Lutz—a bipolar with a criminal record who was sent to St. Mary's as a condition of his probation.
If anyone needed therapy—he was it! Marlee was thinking.
The hospital was dependent on city and state funding and that meant that identified mental patients could not be turned away.
Anyways, where would they send them?

Seattle had its own hands full of homeless drifters, addicts, street people, and a whole host of regular folks whose minds had started to malfunction for one reason or another.

Sign of the times. Marlee was well aware that she was on the frontline of the crisis.
But this—this was going too far.

She picked up the phone and called Security. Then she memo-ed her supervisor Dr. Don Walker.

If she'd had a husband, she would have texted him.

But, of course, she didn't.

By noon, she'd received a spooky e-mail—probably from the same person, but you never know...

Don't forget me. Im the one who loves you. I need you to say it, say it doctor! Im waiting...

The e-mail was sent from an AOL address that turned out to be from a local internet café.

It was when she got another message under her door that she called the police.

They reviewed CCTV tapes and Marlee got a glimpse of a suspect that might be the guy.

It looked like Judas. He wore his baseball cap backwards and you could see a shock of long blond hair and that chin of his.

The police located Judas not far from the hospital parking lot and brought him in to the station.

He admitted he was on outpatient at St. Mary's Psychiatric Wing and showed them ID.

He was charged with stalking and sending threatening e-mails to the hospital—meaning Marlee.

He cooked his own goose when he told police that he had sent messages to his doctor and that he knew she loved him and wanted to be with him—all of which was delusional nonsense, and when the officer in charge called Marlee, she told him as much.

"Just another day in the Psych ward," said Sam after work when the girls got together at The Watering Hole.
"I don't know how you do it," said Rhonda. "I really don't!"

"Maybe you should've stuck to pediatrics," said Sam.
"Too late now," said Marlee.

The drinks came—along with the chicken fingers and nachos.

"It's creepy that the guy got to your office door and hacked your e-mail," said Sherrie.
"We get weirdoes in our medical office from time to time, but nothing that requires me to call the cops," she added.

There was a moment of awkward silence.

Sam spoke first.
"Ah...the elephant in the room...anybody notice it?"

Bev was not there so Sam felt she could bring up the forbidden topic.

"So what is up with Daniel?" said Rhonda with a mischievous twinkle in her eye.

It caught Marlee off guard.

She just blurted out something.

"Daniel has been laid-off and went to join a fire crew in the mountains. I don't even know if...if..." but she couldn't finish her sentence.

"Oh my gawd!" Sam said. "You think he might be in danger out there? Has he phoned you at least?"

"Once. But that was while they were still getting prepared and stuff like that," said Marlee.

"Does Bev know any of this?" said Sherrie.

"Bev and I had coffee and discussed the matter," said Marlee.

"That doesn't sound like it went too well," observed Rhonda.

"Well, we kind of sorted it out, so anyways..." Marlee said, sounding a bit uncertain.

142

"I guess when you're married nobody wants to hear your sad stories," grumbled Rhonda, the only married one among them.

"Hey! You wanna complain about your wonderful husband—you go right ahead!" said Sam.

"Yeah, he is kind of wonderful," admitted Rhonda.
"How's Jennifer?" asked Marlee.
"Great. She turns thirteen in May."
"Thirteen? She grew up!" Marlee said.
"Yeah. And Rob is eleven this year, so, yeah—they aren't toddlers anymore."

Rhonda showed the girls some photos on her iPhone.

"I always felt that kids are lovely so long as they are somebody else's," said Sam.

"I don't," protested Sherrie. "I just never met the guy I would want to spend the rest of my life with."

"And I had plans with Jarrod," said Marlee with a tinge of bitterness. "Look where that got me!"

"Hey, Marlee," said Sam. "You are young enough to still find a man and settle down and have kids. Don't give up on yourself."

Marlee's answer was to pour another glass of wine and grin as she poured its contents down her throat.

***

Many successful people will point out that they have enjoyed the attention of a mentor—some special person who took the time to make sure you were learning it right, doing it right.

Although Marlee had no such person, she did have a supervisor who was a senior physician in the medical school: Dr. Markham Stouffville.

Dr. Stouffville was a Professor Emeritus at U. Washington as well as Intern Supervisor, and was regarded as an authority on mood disorders and their management.

His 1998 paper on *Affect Control in Bipolarity and Dysthymia* was a seminal paper in the field of mood therapy.

It was surprising, though, that he remembered Marlee—she was just one of hundreds that had passed through the halls of academia.

It was even more surprising when she got an e-mail invitation to dinner with the professor--she could not help but be curious!

Charlene's was an upscale and classy restaurant in downtown Spokane.
Although it had an eclectic menu, it did prime rib rather nicely, and always had generous portions of side dishes, and a Caesar salad to die for.

Marlee had been here once or twice with Jarrod.

"Marlee!" said Dr. Stouffville rising to greet her with a sneak kiss to her left cheek.

"Dr. Stouffville. It is such a pleasure to see you. It's been some time," said Marlee.

"How has Life been treating you? I hear you are doing great work at St. Mary's," he said.

"If it doesn't kill me first," she joked.

The first thing that made her a little uncomfortable is his gaze—he never took his eyes off her. He was even studying her cleavage! Ick!

Dr. Stouffville poured them both a glass of chardonnay from Napa Valley in California.
If nothing else, he had good taste in wine.

"Ah, how's your wife?" Marlee ventured.

"Gone. We separated three years ago and the divorce came through last December."

"Oh, I'm sorry."

"It's better for both of us. She is seeing some dentist and he has money apparently."

It was awkward for a moment.

"I find that my practice at St. Mary's is not what I expected," Marlee began.

"I was hoping to focus on children—and of course I am working with adolescents—but I am called upon more often to attend acute presentations in Emerg. Some of my patients are seriously ill.

Perhaps you have some advice for a newbie!"

His hand reached across the linen tablecloth and rested on hers; she withdrew her hand slowly and discreetly.

"You have the resources of one of the top hospitals at your disposal, Marlee.

And of course—you have *me*."

There was no mistaking that look—he had crossed a line without even blinking and Marlee was in shock.

First of all, this is the second time in a week that a rogue male had insinuated himself on her—right out of the blue.
Secondly, this was a much older man whom she respected and trusted, who now seemed to be hitting on her—again, coming out of left field!
Is Mercury retrograde or something? She wondered.

"I've read your papers," Marlee managed to blurt out hoping to deflect that lascivious gaze.

"I wondered if subsequent clinical experience supports your principal thesis, Dr. Stouffville?"

The doctor was finishing his second glass and the meal had not even arrived yet.

"I have students to follow up on all that," he replied with a whiff of arrogance.

Marlee was desperately thinking of what to say next. But he beat her to it.

"I don't understand why a lovely young lady like you is not married yet," he began.

He was twirling the goblet by the stem in a way that made Marlee even more nervous.

Her 'danger!' alarm was starting to go off and she was now on the defensive.

She wanted to lie to him, throw up smoke and mirrors—anything to push him away.
But that was just not in her nature.

"I've been dating someone—a criminal lawyer," she said. *That is true! I was dating Jarrod; maybe not now but that is irrelevant.*

"A local boy, is he?"

"Yes, yes of course. We have discussed marriage."
Again—not a fib; they DID discuss marriage and buying a house and...dammit! Why am I backed into a corner like this?

148

Just then—as if to answer her unspoken prayer—the food arrived and they began to eat their meal.

Not surprisingly, her veal parmigiana seemed tasteless and the salad limp.

She had a brilliant idea!
She excused herself to the Ladies', and rang up Sam on her cell.

"Sam? Help!" she whispered frantically.

"Where are you?" said Sam.

Marlee filled her in on the details.

"Can you come? Just barge right in. I'll handle the rest," Marlee said.

Dr. Stouffville had eaten half his prime rib and most of his potato when she returned.

"How's the beef?" said Marlee cheerily.

It would take Sam ten minutes to throw on some evening dress and get to the car; then ten minutes to get down to Fort Street and find parking.
That left five minutes to get into Charlene's and find her.

Please hurry!

"Have you got children, Dr. Stouffville? I never asked you."

It worked.

"I've got three," he said, his speech stretching his words a little bit longer than normal as the wine hit him a bit more.

"Marilyn is at UCLA Medical school. Mervin is at Berkeley Law, and Sherrilyn is married to a guy in the service—Navy, actually—and lives in San Diego."

"Oh? Grandkids?"

"I've got two and another on the way. Mervin married a nice girl from the Bay area and they are expecting in November."

That's fifteen…Sam should be here inside of ten, twelve minutes.

"So have you plans to go see them?"

This was like playing pingpong, Marlee thought. Keep 'em busy with fast returns over the net.

But Marlee didn't reckon that the older man had a paddle in his hand too!

"Let me get to the point, Marlee.

I am looking for a—companion, you might say. I don't particularly want to spend my golden years watching TV by myself.

I could offer you many advantages."

Marlee was literally holding her breath.

"I own several properties in the Spokane area, a villa in La Jolla California, and a horse farm in Vermont. Take your pick!"

Marlee was looking at her cell. No text from Sam.

"I am emotionally and mentally stable, have a reasonable sense of humor, and—".

His voice dropped conspiratorially.

"...I'm pretty good in the sack!" he announced.

Marlee spilled the remainder of her second glass on her blouse—right in front.

Again—the angels were hovering nearby because Sam in all her glory rushed up to the table and introduced herself to the good doctor.

"I hope I am not intruding," she said—knowing damn well she *was* and had fully intended to.

"Oh, sit down Sam. I want you to meet a man who has inspired me and been an example to me…"

Marlee was just babbling like an idiot.

The doctor looked annoyed.

Sam ordered a rum and 7UP.

She was not above telling a little lie or two if the occasion called for it.

"Yes, yes, Marlee has told me all about you Doctor Stouffville. It's a pleasure to meet you at last."

Marlee told Dr. Stouffville that Sam worked nearby and they often got together for drinks and wasn't it a nice coincidence that Sam just happened to come to Charlene's tonight and get to meet him.

It was soon clear that the assault on Castle McCowan had failed.

Dr. Stouffville called for and paid the check and excused himself.

"Wonderful seeing you again, Marlee. Keep in touch."

Once it was clear he had left the dining room, Marlee threw herself into Sam's arms.

"I so *owe* you, Sam!"

"What a creepy guy!" Sam replied.

"Was he really someone you worked with before? He needs a new pair of glasses. Those frames went out in 1979!"

They were both giggling and smiling now, and by the time they left it was close to midnight.

Chapter Nine   More Creepy

Every law enforcement officer and every hospital emergency room staffer knew that the full moon always brings the crazies out.

No psychiatric explanation was needed. But it never failed—and this month was no exception.

The first hint of trouble was the call over the intercom for Security to come to Admitting.

Marlee was up to her elbows in paperwork at her office desk.

School officials wanted notes for students who missed class to go to Group; social workers wanted detailed documentation of their clients' prognosis. It was endless!

Code Black. I repeat: Code Black.

Code Black? She had to think for a minute.

Jesus! That's *Armed Intruder*!

Marlee had had enough of intruders and stalkers and dirty old professors.
Just leave me alone, will ya?

But curiosity overcame her common sense and she stepped into the hall that led to a main corridor running from Admitting to the Psychiatry Wing.

What she saw was from a movie.

A guy had taken a hostage at the front and was brandishing a pistol.
Ironically, he was shouting the very thing that Josep Filipchik shouted at his trial.

"Stay away from me!" the man said. "I'll kill her! I'll kill you all!"
He meant it.
He fired a shot that hit an overhead light fixture—showering glass over the scene.

Marlee could see patients cowering beside the furniture--the Admitting Nurse Judy crouched on the floor.

Marlee craned her neck out to see who the captive was—hoping it was not staff.

Maybe it was his wife or girlfriend—someone that had triggered a violent response that was going to end in tragedy.

She did not know the woman—but she knew the guy with the gun!
Randy Gervais.

Another patient with mental problems that were hard to handle—both for the patient and the doctor, who, in this case was Dr. Marlee McCowan.

Shit! Shit!! Why does it have to be one of mine?

There was a policy in the Code of Ethics that said that a doctor must treat a patient who comes to them in distress.

There was also a policy that public institutions like hospitals and clinics that depend on tax dollars cannot turn people away in need of help.

Marlee instinctively went back into the interior of her office to the medicine cabinet that was always locked.
The key was in her middle drawer. Or it was *supposed to be!*
It took her a minute to locate it in her white lab coat pocket.

She was looking for a syringe and a vial. Sedative. Powerful one.

This time she was looking for ketamine— originally developed as a horse tranquillizer.

No sooner that she had shuffled the materials into a bag, than shots rang out down the corridor!

Someone screamed—actually several people—and Marlee heard a walkie-talkie and knew that the police were here.

They had fatally shot Randy Gervais. His hostage—some random visitor—had been released and sat in a chair while a nurse attended to her.

Marlee's shoes crunched in the glass on the floor as she approached the officer.

She felt she had to say something.

"Officer? This is one of my patients. I don't know what provoked him tonight.

I will share with the police department what I know that doesn't violate doctor-patient confidentiality."

The police officer took her card and jotted something in her notebook.

She lingered until the body had been removed and the police had gone.

"Are you all right?" she asked the admitting nurse on duty.

"A bit shaken up," Judy said. "I think I need something stronger than a coffee."

Funnily enough, the Security guy on tonight pulled out a hip flask of whisky and Nurse Judy took a very long pull.

That was teamwork—that was one of the few joys of working in a hospital. Knowing that someone had your back!

It was one-thirty in the morning before Marlee reached her car and started it.

***

The mailbox was full of flyers and real estate agents' listings—so she almost missed the smaller postcard postmarked 'Wenatchee WA' showing a valley scene.
It was handwriting she did not recognize but knew right away it was Daniel's.

Still alive out here. Fire's settled down and I may be home soon. Buy me a beer?
Daniel

Not *'love Daniel'* or *'Miss you terribly, Daniel'*. Marlee sighed.

She noticed a white hair while brushing her teeth. There might have been two.

She was in shock for a moment as she realized time was passing and the woman in the mirror was going to see more wrinkles and more gray hair.

Is this how it's going to go from now on? Just wait for the crowsfeet and drying skin as I learn to enjoy being a spinster? No fucking way!

Marlee rinsed her mouth and turned out the bathroom light and slid into bed.

At work she pawed through her office filing cabinet to find whatever she had on Randy; there was a protocol that once a patient was dead, the file would be sent to Archives and stored for who-knows-how-many years.

Her job was simply to get the file in order, and make a notation on the database that he was 'deceased' and on which date.
Case closed--literally.

Marlee did her rounds on the ward—checking each child, holding a tiny hand or brushing a soft cheek.

She was having a coffee in the staff lounge when her cell beeped.
I'm home, Marlee. Need a place to crash until the girl moves out. A couple of days. Where are you?

'Where am I?' What a dumb question! I'm at work. Is he serious? Wants me to put him up?

Marlee dumped the contents of her mug into the sink and stomped back to her office.

She wanted to call her Mother. Then she realized that this was *her* issue and that she can't go run to Mom whenever something hits the fan.
But there was always Sam and Rhonda and Sherrie and…yes…Bev, too!

Anyone else need a drink? read Marlee's e-mail to the girls.
She got a positive response from all parties so they agreed to meet on Friday.

Friday? But Daniel is here now—on Tuesday!

Six weeks in the bush did nothing to make him un-sexy or un-attractive!
He was tan, had a beard, smelled like smoke and sweat and he had a glint in his eye when he climbed in.

"Sorry." Marlee said. "Traffic."

"Yeah you forget about things like that when you are hundreds of miles from nowhere out in God's Country," Daniel said.

"Do we need to stop to get...supplies?" asked Marlee on the way to her apartment.
Meaning liquor.

"If you have some beer that would be good," said Daniel with a cheerful tone.

"Let's swing by Grant's Groceteria and pick up some things," she replied.

"I have cash," he said awkwardly.

"I have a VISA card," she said--smiling for the first time. "You get to carry the groceries in," she said.

"I forgot how good home-cooking is," he said, pushing back from the table.

"Wait till you try Doris' apple pie," said Marlee, clearing away the dishes. "I have one in the freezer."

"No, no thanks," said Daniel. "I am so stuffed.
Never got quite enough in the fire-camp, what with eighty hungry firefighters all rushing to fill their plates at the buffet."

"I've never had that experience," said Marlee drily.

Ripley lay across Daniel's feet and snored with contentment.

Marlee was rummaging in the linen closet for a sheet and blanket for Daniel—who would be sleeping on the couch.

"Where did you sleep?" she called out from the upstairs.

"In tents—four men to a tent. Cozy," said Daniel.

"Where did you sleep in the Air Force—I never asked you," she replied, coming downstairs with her arms full of bedding.

"I was an officer so we got beds in a Quonset hut. Hot showers. Air-conditioning. The works."

"Yeah, except you could hardly sleep knowing that some guy with a mortar or missile was aiming right at your living quarters," said Marlee.

"There was that, yes. But you get used to it. The shellfire, the pak-pak-pak of the AK47s."

She wanted to tell him she was worried about him out on the forest fire crew.

She wondered why she felt worried about Iraq and his past experiences—when she didn't even know he existed at the time!

"Cheers!" said Daniel raising his glass as he turned to greet her.

"Cheers," said Marlee. "Glad you are back. Uh...safe and sound, I mean."

"We did lost a couple of men on the fire," Daniel confided. "Burning limbs and trees fell on them. Freak accident.
    I saw a tree with fire burning out the heartwood but the outer bark was intact. You didn't know you had a little volcano on your hands until your chainsaw ripped through.
    I saw sparks and flames shooting along the blade of the saw! It was dramatic!"

Marlee studied this man.

He was quite intelligent and seemed to notice and assess what was happening around him under conditions that would make many people wet their pants!

"Will you try to get your job back at the warehouse?" Marlee said.
    She was a practical woman—unlike her mother. Bottom line? Gotta have a job!

"I'm thinking of trying to get a security guard position somewhere. Use my military experience. Maybe better money."

"Good. That's good," she said. Then another thought came to her.

"Do you need to carry a gun? I mean—is it dangerous, with—like—burglaries and break-ins and stuff?"

"Maybe—to both questions."

Daniel pulled at his beer.
"I don't have a problem with packing a gun. I am prepared to shoot somebody if I had to-- but in actual fact--I've had enough shooting and killing in the war to last me a lifetime."

The evening shadows covered his face and Marlee switched on the lamp.

"I didn't mean to..." but he cut her off.

"No, it's cool. Am I sleeping here on this couch?" he said.

"Is it okay we don't sleep together right now?" said Marlee.

"Hey, I don't expect anything from you, Marlee. You've been my best friend since I came west."

"If you need anything, just come knock on my door," Marlee stated as she started to climb the staircase.

"Good night," said Daniel.

What if he interprets 'need anything' as sex? Marlee thought as she washed her face.
Why is it I always say things that can get me in hot water?

The next thing she remembered it was morning and Daniel was already up and making coffee.
"Hope you don't mind. I just did it out of habit." Daniel said. He offered the pot.

"Want some?"

Marlee made toast and scrambled, and sat down beside Ripley who was wagging like crazy. Poor dog had really missed his master.

Out of the blue, Daniel asked: "When's your birthday?"

"Ah, in the summer actually," said Marlee.

"That would make you a Cancer sun-sign?" said Daniel.

"Yes," Marlee said. "I'm a homebody. How come you know some astrology?"

"I did a lot of reading in Iraq when I had the time. We weren't engaging the enemy 24/7, you know. Much of the time was waiting, waiting."

"Well, when's *your* birthday?" she retorted.

"January. I'm a Capricorn. Organized. Ambitious. Aloof...somewhat. Made me a good officer in the Forces. Makes me know what is important and what is not."

His voice took a serious tone.

Am I supposed to be reading between the lines here? Marlee mused.

"I've gotta go to work. You going to just hang out today?" she asked.

"If that's okay," Daniel replied. "Leave me a key and I will walk Rip down by the river. Stretch my legs a bit."

"Fine. I'll finish around 5:30 today. I'll pick up something for dinner. Just make yourself at home," she said and opened her car door.
I'm doing it again!
'Make yourself at home'.

What am I thinking? What if he decides that word' home' means my place? My space?
Jesus! I've got to learn to keep my mouth shut!

Dinner turned out to be steak and salad.

Marlee was used to cooking just for herself so she had to be a bit imaginative now that she had a dinner guest—a hungry man!

"What did you do today?" Marlee began.

"Not much," said Daniel. "I read the classifieds to see what kind of work is out there."
"You have to go online nowadays," said Marlee. "That's where the hot jobs are."

"Maybe I should go back to school?" he said. "They've got a diploma course for security guards and private investigators I think.

I received the equivalent of a bachelor degree in the military but I need a specific focus for my career."

"Oh, so you *are* thinking big, Sergeant Briar? That's very good!" Marlee said.

"I'll be thirty next January 5th," he said. "Time to get my shit together as a civilian. Time to have a plan."

"Look into it, Daniel," she said. "You've got a lot to offer. You're not some dumb GI."
He looked at her.
"Sorry. I didn't mean that to come out the way it sounded."
"No. I get it. There are guys who are ruined after their service in the military. Alcoholics. Suicides. I've seen them all."

"Want another beer?" she said.

"No. I'm going to turn in early if you don't mind."
Marlee bade him 'good night' and went upstairs.

***

"But he *did* go back to his apartment," said Rhonda.
It was Friday and the joint was jumping with music and people.

"Yes. He didn't even have a suitcase. But I could see he was glad to be back in his old digs. I think in some ways he's a private person—likes his privacy," said Marlee.

The elephant in the room was a baby one this time—and anyways, Bev was there--so better to ignore any naughtiness altogether.

"Did I tell you about the shooting in the Admissions Dept.?" said Marlee deftly changing the topic.

"No! Are you kidding? Where were *you*?" they all said at once.

Marlee told them the tale in lurid detail; the girls all clucked that nothing that exciting ever happens at *their* workplace.

"Maybe I should switch my specialization to something other than psychiatry," she said.
"Maybe I should just get another career—like organic farming or something."

They all laughed and once again were like old times—keeping each other on their feet through good times and bad.

"My birthday is coming, by the way," Marlee said. "Is there anybody who still needs ideas about what to get me?"

"OMG," said Sherrie. "You are one year older, Marlee. Maybe I should knit you socks or something. You're going to be an old lady soon!"

"Yeah," said Bev. "In two years you will be *thirty*. Definitely over the hill!"

"I will get you whatever my credit card can tolerate," said Sherrie firmly.

"Yeah. What do you *want*?" asked Rhonda.

"Truth be told," said Marlee, "I want three weeks in Hawai'i, but I'll take San Diego or Puerto Vallarta instead.
I need a break from all the insanity!"

"That's why you should give up medicine and do farming," said Bev.

"What about my 401-K? How do I save for retirement?" said Marlee jokingly.

"We all want the answer to *that* question," Sam said.

In the ladies' room, Marlee had the thought that it would be nice if Daniel got her something for her birthday.

A cake. A card. Anything.

Then she realized that Daniel may not even know her birthday is coming in just a few days.

Or worse—may not really care.

***

Of all the people she didn't expect to call, Ricki was right up there with the President of the United States.

"Can we have coffee, Marlee? I really need to talk to you," she said.

Marlee wanted to say 'go fuck yourself' or something similarly nasty, but found herself saying 'sure' and arranging a time to meet.

Ricki looked like a dog's breakfast.
No makeup, bags the size of balloons under her eyes.

Marlee could see she was no older than she herself was—maybe a year younger.
But she looked forty and obviously things with Jarrod had not been working out.

To Marlee's surprise and embarrassment, Ricki started to cry as soon as she sat down in the coffee shop.

"Why didn't you tell me he was like this?" she blubbered.

"Ah, well, you made a point of telling me that you were stealing him for yourself—so I didn't get much of a chance to warn you, Ricki."

Marlee was stirring her latte and sipping the foam.

"He is a total prick!" said Ricki.

Marlee agreed—but said nothing and continued to drink.

"First of all, he promised me that it was going to be a long-term thing. He said he was going to buy a house in the country..."

Marlee couldn't shut up now.

"Funny," she said. "He told me the same thing! House out in the valley, lots of space and fresh air."

Ricki was blowing her nose but clearly listening.

"I told him I wanted to go to the college and study culinary arts," Ricki said.

"He said 'What the hell for?' and I said 'Because I like cooking' and he said 'Fine, but you pay for it yourself!'"

"Is that how he treated *you*?" asked Ricki.

It was a rhetorical question, so Ricki went on.

"I told him I wanted a baby," she continued.

"He said 'I don't,' just like that. Like there was something wrong with wanting a baby, or a family."

"He *can* be heartless once you scrape off the slick and charming exterior," said Marlee.

Marlee decided to be bolder.
"Is he sleeping with someone else?"

Ricki looked like she had just stepped barefoot in a pile of warm dog-shit.

"Huh? You think it's *that*? I never even considered..."

"Just asking, that's all," said Marlee.

Ricki started bawling again.

Marlee thought what a waste of time it is to be crying over a scumbag like Jarrod.

"So where did he leave it, Ricki? Did he say it's over?

Why are you coming to see me? I can't tell you anything that's going to help you.

He's cruel and arrogant and that's just the way he is.

You have to decide if is he worth it—or not," said Marlee finally.

"He said maybe I should look for another place," said Ricki sniffling.

"Have you got a job?" asked Marlee.

"I work in a real estate office and they treat me pretty good," she said.

"Well, that's handy," said Marlee sarcastically. "They will have a direct line on rental accommodation—making your job of finding a new apartment a lot easier.

Look--I'm sorry for what's happened to you, Ricki, but I can't do much more for you than buy you a coffee and listen."

"That's okay. I really appreciate you taking the time," said Ricki.
"And I'm really sorry for what I did to you, Marlee," she said.

"Maybe it's true that what goes around comes around," Ricki muttered to herself.

Marlee paid the waitress and put on her coat.

"You take care, Ricki."

She found her car on 5th Street with a parking ticket under the windshield wiper.

Rats! Speaking of bad karma!

She decided to head to the grocery on the way home, and to call her mother—who had been feeling dizzy and tired lately.

She needed a hug from Daniel. But Daniel was going to have to offer that *himself.*

Chapter Ten   A Birthday Surprise

In fact, Daniel had not forgotten her birthday. He had got her something special that he found in the mountains at a local craft shop.

"What *is* it?" said Marlee, smiling in delight.

"It's a bear. It's hand-carved by an old native man. Yakima or Nez Perce, I forget."

"It's lovely, really, Daniel. Thank you."

"Happy birthday, Marlee. Uh…27th?"

"28th."

The waiter brought the drinks.

"So, here's to the most beautiful woman I know," said Daniel, raising his glass.

"Thank you," she replied and gently touched her glass to his. "I didn't know you liked wine," she said.

"Only in certain company," Daniel said with a grin.
Why is it that when a man grins he either looks wolfish or handsome? she thought.

"So what are you going to do for the rest of the summer," Marlee inquired.
"I hope not more forest-fire fighting?" There's better ways to make a living."

"Actually, I am taking an online course in Security and Protection from Spokane College.
And I've landed a job at one of the warehouse facilities as a night watchman."

"Oh, really? I know you mentioned 'security guard' in passing but I wasn't sure you were serious."

"Like you said: my military background gives me an edge and I'm handy with firearms and I have no criminal record."

"That's great, Daniel!" Marlee held out her glass for a refill.
"This is a nice Chardonnay, by the way."

She was starting to relax and enjoy herself for the first time in who-knows-how-long.

"This one is from the Napa Valley north of San Francisco," he said.
"Vintners in California have really perfected their art over the last few decades. Of course they have the terroir and the sun—which doesn't hurt."

Daniel was looking at her with those eyes she had secretly dreamed of—not bedroom eyes, exactly, but eyes full of warmth and affection.

"The only downside to this gig," he said, "is that I have to work nights—like evening shift and graveyard until, like, 8 a.m."

"Is that permanent?" asked Marlee. "When will I get to see you?"

She was letting her feelings show and felt no inclination now to hold them back.

"I don't know," he said. "This kind of work is always gonna be at strange hours."

He looked down at his steak and furiously cut at it.
He felt Marlee's gaze on him.

"Well, maybe it's not for too long, maybe you can get a security position with a day shift later on."

"We will work something out," he said--and those blue eyes looked right into hers and she felt her pulse jump.
"Can you? Please?"

She was in a waterfall and going over -- surrendering to its surge.

"Sleep with me tonight," she said.
"If you want me to."
"I want you to," she said.

***

She turned off all the downstairs lights and hurried up to her bedroom and slipped into a sheer nightie.

Daniel climbed the stairs and was commenting on the art she had hung on the stairwell—mostly watercolors of landscapes with water and wildflowers.

"You have a nice collection here, Marlee," Daniel said reaching the door of her bedroom.

"I always thought water color was so classy because it is so much more difficult to execute that pushing paint around on a canvas with a palette knife or a brush."

"Shut up," she said suddenly and pulled his mouth down on hers.

He shucked his pants and pulled his shirt over his head without undoing any buttons.

He was hard and she pushed his jockey shorts down as he lay on top of her.

Marlee moaned as he entered and began to push and lift in a rhythm.

He kissed her neck under the hairline and buried his face in her hair as he climaxed.

She felt the energy as she went over the waterfall once more—this time it was with her whole body and she clenched and released and then lay back—spent and happy.

When she awoke, Daniel was in the shower and was singing a Steve Perry song.

Marlee stretched her arms way over her head and then swung her legs out and slipped into her robe.
Saturday. The best day of all.

Marlee decided to prepare some breakfast while Daniel walked Rip.

There was a park not far from her apartment in Rockwood about a ten-minute walk.
Although the city by-laws discouraged it, dog owners would let their dogs off their leash so they could run; every dog owner knows dogs need to have a chance to stretch their

legs and burn off some energy—just like children.

Daniel had trouble remembering exactly what happened next.

Perhaps Rip was chasing another dog and they ran out into the street. Maybe it was the other way around.

Brakes screeched and a dog yelped and it was immediately clear to Daniel that Ripley had been struck by a car driving way too fast for a side street like this.

The driver of the SUV was examining his grille and scratching his head.

Daniel was shouting and swearing.
"You killed my dog! What if that had been a child crossing?"

A small crowd gathered—parents with kids and dog owners, pretty much everyone that had been in the park.
"Should we call the police?" one woman asked.

"I didn't expect that, I didn't even see him till it was too late," the driver was explaining.

Daniel knelt over Rip's body and covered him with his jacket.

The police *did* arrive as someone *did* put in a call.

They charged the driver with careless driving, while one officer helped him carry Rip to the roadside, asking what happened.

"It's also my fault," he said. "I had him off leash and—then this happens."

"That's why we have the by-law, sir," said the officer. "Are you okay getting home?"

"Yeah, thanks, officer."

Daniel just huddled over his dog—still stunned and for a moment clueless what to do next.

He called Marlee.

"I'll be right there. Let me call the vet and tell him we are bringing him in," she said.

The vet said he would ensure the dog would be properly handled—meaning 'cremated' and his remains disposed of.

"Oh, Daniel," she said on the way home, "it's not your fault. He was being a *dog*. If anyone's to blame, it's that stupid driver. I'm glad he was charged. Did he even apologize to you?"

Daniel looked out the car window at some distant spot in the sky.

"Do you want to go to the SPCA and see if they have a puppy in need of a home?" she said.

"No. But thanks for trying to cheer me up. I just need some time to deal with this."

The whole rest of the weekend was low-key as they both felt the loss.

Worst of all from Marlee's perspective was that Daniel kind of pulled into his shell-- leaving her feeling left out—kind of powerless or irrelevant somehow.

She was only trying to help, but when men are upset they just retreat like that, she reminded herself.

At least he wasn't hostile like Jarrod used to be.

She wondered if that is what happened to Ricki. She was pretty messed up over what had happened between her and Jarrod.

Daniel ate in silence and didn't ask to stay the night.

Marlee kissed him gently at the door—and he was gone into the night, like a candle blown out.

Chapter Eleven   Close To You

Marlee needed her friends. She needed at least two glasses of wine.

"Cheers!" said Rhonda.

"What's been happening in your life, Marlee?" asked Sherrie.

"Nothing new—which is not making me happy, guys," Marlee said.

"Things are not settled at work and you're still single," said Bev. "Welcome to your Thirties!"

"I know what I want, but it just floats there—slightly out of reach," said Marlee.

"Look, Marlee. Here's what you are still not understanding.
    The Good Life isn't just going to drop in your lap.
    You've had your share of ups and downs, but whatever it is you truly, *truly* want—you will have to create, maybe from scratch."
    Bev was looking at her, and the other two were looking at Bev.

She looked old these days—tired and worn out. But her eyes were piercing and her voice steady.

"I might be wrong, Marlee, but I have always thought of you as a 'family' kind of person. I think that is because 'family' means stability, means continuity. You are a giver—and you are missing that centerpiece of husband and family that would draw out the best in you."

Marlee blinked back a tear.

"You need a plan, Marlee," Bev went on.
"You need a set of goals that are time-sensitive. Like—by Thanksgiving, I will be engaged to a wonderful guy.
It *has* occurred to me that this town might be a little short on Prince Charmings.
Have you considered moving to...a bigger city? Someplace with culture and night life and more eligible and suitable men?"

Sherrie got into it.

"You can do better than trying to get this ex-serviceman back on his feet, Marlee. No offence—but is he really worth investing your time and energy in?"

Marlee was quiet. She knew she was getting honest advice from her best friends and it was meant well.

And maybe they were right.

"Hey? How about I quit my job and we move to San Diego, Marlee?"

This was coming from Bev who had been a voice of Reason for years for Marlee.

"How about we order another bottle and think about that," said Rhonda—perhaps to lighten the mood a shade.

"OK," said Marlee. "Let's do a little game. I go around the table and ask each of you in turn what you would do if you were in my place.

Starting with you, Rhonda."

"I would relentlessly hunt down a guy that fulfills my checklist and tie him down before he knew what hit him," Rhonda replied.

Everyone laughed.

"How long is the checklist?" Marlee asked.

"Seven pages," quipped Bev. "Not including footnotes."

The girls were having that time they so badly needed—a time of trust and laughter and mutual confirmation.

"Sherrie?"

"I agree you don't have the luxury of time to waste. And why should you? These are your best years, supposedly.
You need to know *exactly* what you want and get that for yourself—whether it's here in Spokane or some other place—doesn't matter.

If I knew someone—or *knew* someone that knew some nice guy—believe me, Marlee! I would drag you over there right now.

Like I'm one to talk! I thought about marriage and kids and decided life is a whole lot simpler if I'm cooking just for one."

"Speaking of—can we order some food?" said Bev.

It was Wing Night so they ordered about four pounds—with fries and coleslaw.

"Your, turn, Bev," said Marlee.

"I totally get how you feel torn between duty at work and duty to your family, to your mother. This is why everybody in social media raves on about 'work-life balance'.

This is nothing new. Only we all grew up where fathers went to work and mothers stayed home and kids ate their vegetables and did their homework in the evening.

That's all changed.

Women are out there on their own—many still having to take care of someone and manage a career at the same time. But the social supports are gone.

Now it's 'Do your own thing, walk the talk,' or whatever talk show hosts say these days."

"Well you're not answering Marlee's question," Sherrie teased.

"What I am saying is I have no fucking clue," Bev admitted. "All I have is you guys and this glass of zinfandel.

For now, I am grateful for having even that.

I don't honestly know what I would do with a husband if I *had* one."

"Well," Marlee said putting down her napkin, "I *want* one.

I want a home with swings in the backyard and a barbecue on the deck.

I want my kids in the family room playing games with their friends, and I want my mother to see her grandchildren around her.

I want a man that wants only me and knows how to show it."

"Amen," the girls clinked glasses one last time.

***

"Mom? Can I come over for dinner?"

It had been another brutal day at the hospital and Marlee could not face cooking or even eating out.

Besides, she wanted her mother. It was just that kind of day.

"Hi, honey!" Doris embraced her daughter and closed the front door tight and turned the deadbolt.

"Wash up and come down. I will serve." Marlee did as she was told.

"Mmmm…you do roast chicken so well, Mom!" Marlee said.

"I learned it right the first time," her mom said with a smile.

"You can do it, Marlee—you just have no time."

After dinner, they sat on the couch together.

"Mom. Can I tell you something?"

"Of course. What is making my baby girl's eyebrows and forehead all wrinkly this evening?"

"Mom, I might be pregnant. My period is three days late. And I'm not usually late."

Doris shifted and pulled her legs up and tucked them under her.

"You mean—Daniel?"

"Yes."

"Does he know?"

"No, Mom, I didn't mention this to anyone. If I am pregnant, I have some tough decisions to make," she said.

Doris pulled a cozy throw from the armchair and wrapped Marlee up in it.

"I didn't know you two were—."

"We're not. I mean, we only did it once—on my birthday. I just kind of lost control. I wasn't expecting anything would happen."

"You have to tell him, darling!"

"What difference will it make? He has not done anything to suggest that he really wants a commitment, that he wants a life with me.

It's almost like a cat-and-mouse game with him. He just pops up from time to time but never shows what he is really thinking."

"What do you *think* he is thinking?" asked Doris.

"I wish I knew, I really do. I haven't had the guts to ask him.
I guess I'm afraid that will drive him away—and he's already nearly beyond reach.

Pregnancy would be the kiss of death for us.
It would mess up my career and without a strong partner in my life, I just couldn't...I just don't know what I'd do."

"You know I will help you raise her...or him," said Doris.

"That's not the point, Mom."

Marlee adjusted her position and put her feet out on the ottoman.

"I don't want to raise a child without a proper environment—I mean, a father on scene.
And right now, Daniel is looking anything *but* a father and husband."

"Sleep over for a few days. Let's see what develops. Then we can decide, okay Marlee?"

"Sure, thanks Mom."

Soon they turned out the lights and headed up to bed.

Marlee had troubled dreams. Usually she was lost but this night she had a sense she would find the road again.

***

Marlee's period came the next day and gave her a chance to catch her breath.

But still—what about the conversation she had with the girls? What about 'relentlessly' pursuing her goals of husband and stable life?

It was becoming all she could think of.

There was no other way. She had to confront Daniel—even if it meant backing him into a corner.

It was time to shit, or get off the pot!

They were sitting in Marlee's living room.

"I thought you loved me?"

Daniel fidgeted.
"I do. Don't drag it out of me. I have a lot of things on my mind."

"And I am just one of those things?" Marlee shot back.

"I'm confused. I don't have a clear plan of action and my feelings for you aren't letting me get my head clear, Marlee."

"I care about you, Daniel. I believe we could have a future if we could only be on the same page with it.
That means commitment, a mutual agreement to build a life together. Never mind the other things.

You have to make up your mind that you-- Daniel Briar—want to be with me—Marlee McCowan—for keeps. No 'buts'. I need to hear it from your heart as well as your lips, Daniel."

To her surprise that made Daniel smile.

It was not a supercilious smile, but a smile that made his eyes crinkle at the corners.

It was a smile that told Marlee she had hit something solid in him.
It was at that moment she realized they had a chance.

Forest fire season had started early this year in the Pacific Northwest. On the whole west coast of North America actually.

There were fires already out of control in greater Los Angeles, and in Santa Barbara. There were hundred of acres in Washington State in the Cascade range burning so bad they could be seen from Space on weather satellites!

Across the border in British Columbia and Alberta, huge fires were threatening small communities and destroying thousands of dollars of good pine and Douglas fir.

In next-door Idaho there were evacuation orders for ranchers and residents of wilderness areas that drove refugees as far south and west as Spokane.

"Don't even *think* it!" Marlee said speaking on the phone to Daniel.

"It's good money," countered Daniel. "Plus I know the routine."

"You'll be all alone, in danger—and I'll be all alone at night wondering if I locked the door and set the alarm.
 I don't want to live like this, Daniel. I want a man who stays home at night. I want you here with me.
 Did everything I said the other night just go in one ear and out the other?"

"There's a small wrinkle. My old air force buddy Rex is in town. I told him to come out to Spokane and damned if he didn't do just that!
 I told him about the forest service contract and he's in! He wants to leave this week. Of course he's broke and needs the money and I don't have any to give him.

It'll be just for a few weeks, Marlee."

There was a slight pause and then the line went dead.

Marlee threw her phone into her bag, locked the door, and started the twenty-minute drive to the hospital.

She shoved the CD into the dashboard player and turned it up until the bass shook the windows.

She nearly collided with an ambulance inbound to Emerg –didn't even hear it.

This was Thursday June 6. The news said fires were even a threat to their city of Spokane.

Nowhere was safe.

Part Three   By Choice

Chapter Twelve   Close Calls

Daniel didn't call later, or even the next day.

Marlee decided that he really *had* gone with Rex to fight fires and prove whatever he had to prove.
She didn't understand yet pretended she didn't want to. It was what it was.

There were plenty of patients in need of Marlee's patient attention.
She was reminded that childhood was not easy—and for some—an exceedingly challenging time.

Parents were often unaware of how their child suffered through sickness, injury, loss, or conflict at school.
It was only recently that 'bullying' was finally acknowledged as a 'thing' that required adult intervention on a broad social scale.

Depression and suicide among children was rising alarmingly but people seemed to think there were no real solutions—or even answers.

As a psychiatrist, she knew better.

She barely had time to grab a sandwich and coffee in the canteen when she was paged.

But it was not a patient in distress—it was about her mother!

"Dr. McCowan, this is Dr. Reed in Cardiology. Your mother Doris has suffered a stroke and has been brought in to Emerg and is getting looked at.
You are welcome to come by and help us process her."

Marlee jammed the rest of the roast turkey-on-Italian into her mouth and thrust her cell and wallet into her inside pocket under the lab coat.

"We're sending her for tests," said Dr. Reed when Marlee arrived.

Marlee took her mother's wrist and checked pulse without blinking. I was routine.
But at this moment she didn't feel so much like a physician as a helpless daughter tending to the person on the gurney.

"Mom? Mom-can you hear me?"

"She's not regained consciousness as of yet," the nurse said. "Once the battery of tests are done, we'll take her up to ICU. Do you want me to give you a call when we do that?"

"Please!" said Marlee.

The orderly pushed the gurney toward the south wing where the specialized equipment including EEG and CAT scan machines were situated.

Marlee's pager went off to remind her she was still at work and still had other duties.

She hurried back to Psychiatry to speak to the intake nurse about an urgent case that had just been admitted.

Overdose. Possible suicide attempt. Subject was thirteen, male, no fixed address.

***

Marlee stayed after hours to go over her mother's medical history.

She realized with shock that her mom had not been diligent in annual medical checkups and had not had blood-work done that would reflect her cholesterol and triglyceride levels.

A stroke is a symptom of cardiovascular disease. Millions of Americans are without overt symptoms and this insidious killer waits until it is often too late to do anything about it.

Doris McCowan was a typical case and the doctor in charge would tell her that it could have gone either way—heart attack or stroke.
Either way, arteries were compromised and blood flow restricted—with dangerous results!

Marlee felt awful. She was a physician. She should have been more responsible. Her mom relied on her to keep an eye on her and she failed.
The event just came out of nowhere it seemed.

The tests were just as expected—*arterial occlusion in motor cortex leading to potential partial paralysis...*
Marlee just sat at her desk and cried.

They had moved her to Intensive Care where she could be monitored for the next few days. There was nothing to be done.

Marlee got in her car and drove home. She stopped for some fast food on the way. She was in no mood to prepare anything.

It was only then that she thought about Daniel. Daniel—the only man she had feelings for right now—was out in the forest and in danger, too!

She snapped on the TV news and it was full of details about the massive fires burning in the Cascades, and how the wind was making it worse and the lack of rain was adding to the woes.

"How can you respect me when I don't respect myself for having a steady job?" Daniel had said.

Marlee was trying hard to understand what was in his mind.

Was it shame that drove him to leave her and go off to some god-forsaken place to make a little money?

Why doesn't he see that I respect him for who he is—not what he does? Why can't he see that I make enough to support us until he gets his feet under him?

Should I have said something?

Most of all—why can't he see that I need him?

That I need him to be here with me and hold me at night and tell me Mom will be alright and that he will take care of me today, tomorrow-- and forever?

Maybe he heard her heart crying out after all.

The phone rang—it was an unknown number. She said 'Hello.'

It was Daniel.

"Hey, Marlee! It's me. I just had a strong hunch I should call. My crew is in town getting supplies and I actually have a moment to myself here."

"Daniel!" A flood of tears came suddenly. "Mom had a stroke and is in hospital."

"Oh, wow! Is she going to be okay?"

"I don't think they know yet. But I miss you and I'm scared and I don't like feeling this way. When are you coming *home*?"

The very word resonated in the still moment between her honest statement and his response.

But his words were enough.
"I'll be home soon, darling. This part of the county is under control and they've got a bunch of new guys who can give the rest of us a break."

Marlee tried to get something out--but failed.

"I promise when I come back we will sit down and plan our future together, Marlee. Can you just hold onto that thought?"

Marlee instinctively nodded—then realized her couldn't see her.
"Yes. Daniel. I will."

"I love you, Marlee. I have to go. I will see you soon."

The line went dead but Marlee's heart was beating with new life.

She cleaned up the plate and leftovers, and started the dishwasher.
She felt an energy humming inside her as she straightened the cover on the couch and drew the curtains closed for the night.

She hugged the pillow just as she would hug him when next he lay beside her.
Then, she was asleep.

***

"She's still not conscious," the nurse reported as Marlee asked to see her mom.

"I just want to see her," said Marlee. "Just for a moment."

"This way." The nurse led Marlee down the hall to a semi-private room, and pulled the curtain aside by the bed.

Her mother's hair was more grey and white than she had remembered it, as if she had been away for a long time.

She sat. Her mother's IV tube was tangled among the leads from the monitor that tracked every second, every change in her heart rate and blood pressure.

She took her mother's hand—fragile as a bird, her skin cool and dry.

"Mom? Mom, can you hear me?"

Marlee did not know if she could or not-- but she continued anyway.

"I want you to come back now, Mom. It's time to come back."

Perhaps she just imagined the flutter of her mother's eyelid, but it made Marlee try even harder.

"Mom. It's Marlee. Marlee McCowan. I am your daughter. And I want you to come home."

Again her imagination was playing up.

She was not sure if her mother's grip tightened just a little—or not.

"I love you, Mom. I need you. Please come back to me. I know you can hear me. I can't do it—you have to do it."

"Doctor McCowan, I'm afraid I'm going to send you away now. The neurologist needs her to do some tests and we're going to wheel her down to the exam room. I'm sorry."

"Sure, I'll get out of your way." Marlee reluctantly released her mother's hand and took the elevator back to Ground.

Back in her office she had time to check her email and grab a coffee.

What caught her attention though was the whirring and roar of the rescue helicopter as it passed over the yard outside her window to land on the rooftop.

They didn't hear it often and it always meant that a trauma case from outside city limits was being flown in to the hospital.

Usually it was a serious crash on the highway, or a farmworker crushed by a machine, or a woman in labor who couldn't get to the hospital in time.

She would have ignored it but the intercom said something about fire crew or Forest Service—something that triggered Marlee enough to wander out in the hall and ask somebody at the nursing station what was going on.

"Some serious injuries from the fire crew up on the mountain—had to be flown in. Ask at E.R. if you wanna know, Marlee."

Cheryl B. was somebody Marlee trusted and enjoyed working with. She had over twenty years in as a nurse here and she knew just about everything about everything that goes on at Sacred Heart.

"Did someone call Psych, Dr. McCowan?" The nurse on duty was new and a bit confused.

"No. I mean, not yet," Marlee said.
"I am asking about who was brought in by the helicopter." She sounded and felt a bit lame.

"Ahhh, two men. One with severe burns and one with unspecified injuries."

"Do you have names?" Marlee persisted.

"Ah, Cochrane and Briar."

"*Daniel* Briar?"

"Yes, Daniel Briar. His ID says he lives here in Spokane."

"I *have to* see him!" announced Marlee.

"He's in triage right now. You'll have to wait until they bring him upstairs," the nurse said in her official hospital employee voice.

Marlee was already yards down the hall rushing to the Triage Unit.

"I'm Doctor McCowan," she said breathlessly. "I need to see a male patient who just came in."

Sometimes that worked. Sometimes you could pull rank and flash your badge and get past the rules and red tape.

"Hello, Dr. McCowan. I am Dr. Ali. How can I help you?"

"Daniel Briar. He is a close friend. I just need a word with him. Please Dr. Ali."

"We normally don't—".

"Fuck normally! Just let me see him!"

Dr. Ali led her to a gurney behind a white curtain where Daniel was lying, obviously in pain and already tethered to an IV.

"Daniel. Daniel—it's me. Daniel?"

Daniel opened his eyes and smiled.

"Hi Marlee. How ya doin'?"

"I'm doin' fine. What the hell happened to you?"

"Tree exploded on us—burning inside then shattered when the guy with the chainsaw cut into it. He was burned bad."

"I think he's the other guy the chopper brought in with you.
Where are you hurt?"

"Something is broken, I know it. Just a lot of pain in my chest and arm right now. How did you know I was here?" he asked.

"Woman's intuition," Marlee said. "I will check in on you later. Don't you die on me, Daniel Briar! Don't you dare!"

Daniel managed a grin this time.

Marlee kissed him hard on the lips and brushed his hair back off his forehead.

She picked up two coffees on the way upstairs: one for Cheryl and one for herself.

"Found him."

"Found *who*?" said Cheryl.

"The guy I was looking for. Ah, he's a friend."

"Oh shit! Is he going to be okay?"

He's not the burn victim. That one's been sedated into dreamland and I wouldn't want to be around when he wakes up," Marlee said.

"Want me to do something?" Cheryl said.

"Naw, just be here and drink your coffee.

Now I have two people close to me as inpatients in this hospital: my mother, and my close friend. I honestly don't know what to think."

"Well, I know you well enough to know that you are strong, Marlee. Just sometimes you have to prove it, girl."

"Keep talking, Cheryl! I just don't want to sit in my office staring at the four walls right now!"

"So stay here," Cherl said. "It's kind of a dead day around here anyways."

Then she caught herself.
"Oh, geez, Marlee—I'm sorry. I didn't mean it that way."

Marlee smiled and they both giggled-- because you have to have a sense of humor to work in a hospital or you just won't make it.

Daniel had three broken ribs, a fractured left forearm, and a mild concussion.
Other than that, he was in good spirits when Marlee appeared.

"I've got—"
"I know. I saw the X-rays. The ribs will mend on their own. The cast will be on for up to six weeks," Marlee said, drawing a little

house on his plastered arm. There were two people and a sun in the picture too.

"Guess I won't be going back on the fire," he said. "Hope Rex will be okay."

"I'm sure he has support on the team," Marlee said. "Right now it's *you* that needs looking after, mister!"

"How long will they keep me?" he asked.

"Not long," she answered. "They are short of beds."

"Can I stay at your place for now?" Daniel asked—sounding for all the world like a lost little boy.

"If you behave yourself!" Marlee teased.
She looked briefly over her shoulder then leaned in and kissed his lips.

"You need a shave," she teased.
"I need a decent meal," he countered.

"I'll ask when they are going to release you," said Marlee.

Marlee went up to look in on her Mom—who was doing much better.

"When can I go home, Marlee? The doctors won't say." Doris was sitting up and drinking soup.

"When they think you can manage—I don't know if they know you don't live with me. I think they assume that I will be there to look after you, Mom.

But I'm not sure I can give you the attention you need. We'll have to get you a private nurse or support worker."

"I can walk with a walker they said," Doris said. "I'm mentally fully functional. I'm only fifty-eight, Marlee. I'll be fine."

"There's another small wrinkle," Marlee said quietly. "There's Daniel. He's been hurt and needs to recover. I'm thinking of keeping him at my place. At least for now."

"I won't be any bother, dear," said Doris.

"No. No. That's not my point. I can look after the both of you. Would it be okay if you stayed at my place for the time being?"

"You mean—with you and Daniel? Won't it be a bit crowded?"

"Well that's what I want to know, Mom.

Me? I don't find it crowded. We have two bedrooms upstairs, and two bathrooms. You can have all the privacy you need," Marlee said.

She could see her mother wasn't keen on it.

Marlee began sourcing a caretaker in her head. She had a list somewhere.

"Let's take it one day at a time, Mom. Okay?"

She turned to Doris but Doris was fast asleep and snoring gently.

Chapter Thirteen Two Steps Forward

In her gmail was a short note from Rhonda—asking Marlee to contact Bev.

Marlee wondered by Bev herself had not sent it. She would soon find out.

"Hey, Bev. It's Marlee. What's going on?"

"The doctor says I have a tumor and I have to go into the hospital for a special biopsy.
  Marlee—I'm scared."

"Jesus, Mary and Joseph! When did all this start?"

"I went to my GP for a general checkup and she noticed my white cell count was unusually high on the blood tests.
  She sent me to an oncologist to investigate.

They did a scan of my belly—well, my uterus actually—and there was a shadow in the image that was unmistakable to both the radiologist and the oncologist.
  I have cancer, Marlee."

"Whoa, hold on Bev. There are other possibilities here. Even if it is a tumor—that doesn't mean cancer, *per se*. It could be a cyst or a benign growth, even an ectopic pregnancy for that matter.

Let's just wait for the biopsy to give us more data, huh?"

"You won't leave me alone will you, Marlee? I mean you won't let me die alone...please?"

"Ok. Stop that right now, Bev! You are not going to die and maybe aren't even ill!

I think you need a drink to calm your nerves and I'm thinking I could use one too!

I'll pick you up after work and we'll go give that new wine bar a try. We good?"

"Thanks, Marlee. Thank you. I'll see you at 6:30 outside my building."

***

"This is a Merlot, ladies," said the cute young waiter with the apron who was cradling the bottle so they could read the label.

"Hit me!" said Bev to the man. Marlee nodded vigorously. He poured two glasses.

Marlee reached for the French baguette in the basket. *Can't have an empty stomach and drink wine* she thought.

"What's the difference between Merlot and Malbec?" asked Bev.

"The grapes, I guess," said Marlee.
"We can get them to bring us a carafe of that one for Round 2," she said with a mischievous grin.

"I feel so lost, Marlee. So vulnerable. Like my body betrayed me in middle age."

"Bodies change, Bev. They age. They break down. But they also renew. There are lots of alternatives to our diet and lifestyle that can make all the difference.
Fasting, for example. I find partial fasting over a two week period helps me flush toxins and excess weight without effort."

"You? You have the body of a goddess, Marlee. Fasting? Yuck! I can't imagine deliberately not eating," said Bev.

"Well our bodies reflect what we eat and what we believe. And evidence suggests that they hold negative emotions in our cells and organs. That is one theory of where cancer originates."

"I guess being a doctor you have to know all that stuff about disease. That would creep me out," said Bev.

"Excuse me?" Bev said to the waiter passing. "Could we have a half liter of Malbec to try?"

"Of course, madam. That's why we are a wine bar and offer many varietals. Do you want French? Or Australian?"
"You choose!"
"Fine. I'll be back in a moment."

"Nice butt," said Bev watching the waiter with the apron disappear.

"See? That's a good attitude to have. Look at the good things in life!" said Marlee.

"I wanted to say something, Marlee," Bev said. "I wanted to apologize. I realize I made a mistake by hustling Daniel off to bed.
I didn't think of you. I thought of myself.

It was only later that it occurred to me that you would have been—and *were*—hurt by that action."

"It caught me by surprise, that's all," Marlee said.
"Anyhow it's in the past. Daniel and I are getting serious and that's what I want."

"Tell me you forgive me, Marlee."

"Of course I do."
"No, I *mean* it. I need you to forgive me."

Bev was looking right at Marlee. She didn't even notice Mr. Cute place the new carafe and two fresh glasses in front of her.

Marlee looked at her longtime friend.

"I *do* forgive you, Bev. Okay?"

Bev let some tears slide down her face.

"I don't want to die with that on my conscience," she blubbered.

"You're not dying, Bev!" Marlee dabbed Bev's cheeks and eyes with a tissue.
"For heaven's sake—let's try this Malbec and stop all this morbid talk."

***

It did make Marlee think, however, about the people she had lost. Ranee...her Dad...
She decided she was not willing to lose her Mother too.

"Mom? I'm coming over. Shall I pick something up on the way?" She started her trusty little Mazda and stopped to get a barbecue chicken at the market.

Marlee had temporarily hired a PSW to stay with her mother in the daytime and it was gratifying to see that Doris had graduated from a walker to a cane.

"You can send that girl home, dear," said Doris. "I am managing just fine."

"Well, I am glad to hear it, Mom. However, I *am* a doctor and I need to be sure there is no sudden relapse that might put you at risk."

"When your Father passed it was so sudden—one day to the next. He felt unwell and went to bed and...and I couldn't wake him in the morning."

"It wasn't your fault, Mom. He had a heart attack. Thousands of Americans have heart disease, and many of them go undiagnosed."

"I should have called somebody. I didn't. If my mother had been alive, I could've called *her.*"

"Mom--stop it! Dad's death was a product of his job stress and ridiculous smoker's habits—I mean he smoked up to four packs a day!

Medicine has taken far too long to lay the blame where it belongs--on the tobacco companies. Don't get me started!"

"I'll make the mashed potatoes—you serve the bird, dear." Doris drained the pot and added a little milk, butter and salt and pepper, then mooshed the whole thing with the ancient potato masher that had been in their family for years.

"Daniel gets out of the hospital tomorrow," Marlee said over dinner. "I think they kept him longer because he suffered a mild concussion and wanted to be sure that wasn't going to be a problem.

"Is he staying with you then?" said Doris.

"I want him to," Marlee admitted.
"He can be so darn stubborn!"
Marlee smacked the table with the flat of her hand so loud it startled her.

"What will he do? He can't fight forest fires his whole life," Doris said.

"He plans to study to get his Private Investigator license," said Marlee.

"With his military background, he can fast-track through the home study program and write the qualifying exam.
He reckons there is lots of work out there."

"Can he work with the police or sheriff's office?"

"Not directly. But he is free to assist or investigate for private companies, lawyers, insurance companies—he has more freedom than police do when it comes to choosing clients and cases," said Marlee.

"Maybe it's good then, Marlee. He will protect you from burglars and muggers and all that street trash that shows up in the news--or in your Emergency Room at Sacred Heart!"

"I don't feel myself to be in danger, but I guess you're right, Mom—it's not safe after dark in this town."

"Now you're acting like you have some sense. Something you got from your Father."

Marlee felt that her Mother wanted to say more. Maybe touch the taboo subject—Ranee.

But she hugged her as she left—advising her to lock the deadbolt and leave one light on all night.

Her car was parked a few doors down and Marlee was aware of the sounds and smells of the rain-slicked street as she got into her car.

Maybe her Mom was right—it wouldn't hurt to have a big strong man as a bodyguard. He could even carry groceries.

***

With his left arm in a sling, however, Sgt. Daniel Briar was not going to be carrying anything heavier than a toothbrush for the next few weeks.

"If you let me register with your VISA card, I'll pay you cash once the government puts my final Forest Service check in the bank."
Daniel was online and getting excited about the PI course that had been recommended by somebody he met on the fire brigade.

"Later. Just get in and download the materials. I'm curious about what they want you to learn. Like, investigative techniques and stuff," said Marlee.

Marlee snugged up beside Daniel on the sofa and threaded her arm through the space between his cast and his ribs.

"Oww," said Daniel.

"Oh, gosh, I forgot it was the ribs on your left side. Sorry honey!"

"You never called me that before," Daniel remarked.

"Oh it just popped out. Don't take it seriously," Marlee teased.

"This is a piece of cake," Daniel was saying. "They give you three months to complete this—I can do it by the time my cast comes off!"

"Are you so clever?" asked Marlee.

"Watch me!" Daniel said. "I can write the exam in two months—latest!"

"Fine by me," she said. "But then what?"

"Then I hang out my shingle—or whatever it is that you do—and get some clients and buy a black Dodge with a lot more horsepower than your little putt-putt out there."

"Zoom-zoom," she countered.

"I will need to get a Conceal Carry permit and a gun. Need to find a club or range to practice. Wanna learn to shoot?"

"Not immediately," Marlee said. "Shall we make some dinner?"

***

There was a letter on her desk that looked very official—it was from the hospital and it was marked 'CONFIDENTIAL'.

Marlee tore it open. It was from the Board of Governors and was signed by the executive vice-president—who approved all the hiring and firing at Sacred Heart.

They weren't firing her, however. Not today. The letter was an offer of promotion to Acting Head of Child Psychiatry at her work.

Later, Marlee couldn't recall whether it mentioned salary or not. It was all a blur.

She wanted to tell somebody. At the same time, she wanted to hold onto it—keep it to herself. Just for a day or so.

She went down to the canteen for a coffee. She passed Cheryl who called out to get her a Large Cappuccino. Done.

"So how's the family doing?" said Cheryl.

Marlee wasn't sure if she meant her mother Doris--or her mother, *plus* Daniel.

"Everybody is mending nicely," said Marlee, trying to slide out of the innuendo in Cheryl's voice.
"You getting holidays this summer?" continued Cheryl in her skillful small talk way.
"You know, I never even thought of it!" said Marlee.

It was true. If she had time coming to her, it was the last thing on her mind.

"My husband's retiring this year," Cheryl went on. "He gets severance pay that gives us enough to take a trip somewhere."

"Where would you go? Italy?"

"Hell no—Disney World," said Cheryl. "I just *loved* Johnny Depp in Pirates of the Caribbean. They have that in Orlando."

"Sounds good to me," said Marlee. "I gotta get back to some paperwork. Thanks for chatting, Cheryl. And congrats on your husband's retirement."

Marlee reflected on the fact that Cheryl had been working here for 29 or 30 years already. Time to retire. What a nice thought!

She read the letter again. Then three more times!

The scope of her duties would double—or even triple.
The workload would be punishing.

She would be responsible for the whole department and its fifteen doctors and nurses, dozens of chronic and acute patients, overseeing the pharmacy, writing endless reports to her superiors, as well as to state and local authorities, physicians and attorneys.

The core issue, of course, was *'am I ready?'*

She had been merely an intern just one year ago. Then had a frenetic fall and winter just managing sessions and caseload.

Somewhere in there was a little happy cloud in a blue sky with 'Home and family' written on it. *What about that?*

Decision time.

Chapter Fourteen   One Step Back

As the weather started to cool off--so did the seasonal work--and the streets of Spokane were filling up again with unemployed or outright homeless men.

Rex Randall was one of them. It didn't take him long to look up his old buddy Daniel Briar.

"Hey Daniel. Wanna go have a couple of beers?" Rex was at a pay phone.

Daniel was looking over some files the D.A. had sent him.
"Sure. Meet you at The Watering Hole around five.
Glad to see you made it back from the fire in one piece. Maybe you heard *I* came back in an ambulance. Tell you all about it later, man."

Daniel scribbled a sticky note for Marlee and placed it on the mirror beside the front door.

Daniel and Rex were part of a cohort of veterans who drifted from town to town, taking whatever work was available.

Their combat experiences overwhelmed many of them physically and psychologically.

They were all dependent on the Veteran's Administration for medical care, financial support, and a sense of connection with ordinary American life that had been stripped away once they shipped out to some foreign destination to serve their country.

They were largely ignored by the world as it rushed by in the glamor of news and scandals and hype.

They came back wounded in body and soul, hardly noticed and rarely shown gratitude for their service.

They were invisible.

The lucky few that had spouses or families waiting received a better reception.

But for men like Daniel Briar and Rex Randall—the days of their lives were spent in impoverishment in every sense of that word.

"Hey, buddy!" Daniel said, shaking Rex' hand and briefly hugging him.

"You look pretty good yourself—tell me about what happened to you," Rex said, as a pitcher of cold beer arrived.

"I was up on the ridge and Andy White was cutting through a big Douglas fir, when sheets of fire and sparks shot out along the cut—and when that tree came down it exploded like a firecracker. One slab creased my ribs and left side, one took that Yakima Indian fella and heaved him right over the cliff, and one fried another guy who ended up in Sacred Heart along with me. I never thought about how trees burn—up, inside, from the roots until they are volcanoes waiting to blow up."

Daniel emptied his glass and refilled it to the rim—then drank that.

"Son-of-a-bitch!" said Rex. "I was way down the draw and didn't even hear about this."

"It'll be my last fire, that's for sure," said Daniel. "I finished up studying for my Private Investigator's license, got myself a gun and a car, and I'm in business, brother."

"Can you deal me in? I'm good with a gun, and you can explain the law as we go along," said Rex reaching for the second pitcher of Miller High Life.

"Not sure, Rex. First of all, you gotta have no criminal record—and you *do*."

"That's ancient history. Aggravated assault. I did my time.

Anyhow, the State of Washington ain't gonna poke the police files of Dayton Ohio. Different jurisdiction."

"Number two is—I hate to say this Rex--but you still have a drinking problem. A serious one.
You were going to bed in the fire camp with a bottle of bourbon for company. That alone could've had you suspended, and maybe charged."

"I can handle my liquor, Daniel. You know that."

"I know—but the State Licensing Board may not see it that way."

"Thirdly, you need to study for several months to pass the Board exam; how long has it been since you've been *near* a book?"

"I got you, old buddy! But *you* know the stuff I need to know. Just open my hood and pour it in!"
Rex was grinning. He had his paycheck from the Forest Service and the beer was flowing good tonight.

"I wanna help you, Rex, don't get me wrong. But there's only so much I can do. I've started to turn my life around since I came out here. You have to do the same."

Daniel changed the subject.

"How about I ask the warehouse guy if he needs a night watchman. Pay's decent—nothing to do but check doors and wave a flashlight around. What d'ya say?"

"I say...I say I gotta have several more beers to think about it."

"Sure thing, Rex. I'm buyin'--so be my guest!"

***

"So what's going to happen, Daniel? Is he going to move in with you, keep you company?"
Marlee was just getting warmed up.

"For the first time in *years*, you have a shot at a *future*—a career, a relationship.
You want to throw that away over someone from your past?" She had an edge to her voice.

"I am loyal to my friends, Marlee. What's wrong with that?"

"Rex is not your friend, Daniel. He's a ghost from your past who will cling to you because you are all he's got.

But he's an alcoholic and—I'm sorry to say this—he's going nowhere.
He doesn't have what *you* have, Daniel.
He's on the street and unless he has an epiphany about his own future, he will *stay* there!"

Daniel shifted uncomfortably on the couch but continued to look at her.

"But Rex isn't really the problem.

It's *you* Daniel--and all the things in your head and heart that you somehow forgot to share with me, leaving me lonely and scared and wondering what *my* future is going to be!"

Daniel laid his hands on his lap and breathed out and there was nothing but silence hanging like smoke in the room.

"I've thought about this moment, when I was all out of excuses, nowhere to run," he began. "I wondered why I seem to want to run from you.
So I'm going to say this in the way it makes sense to me," he said softly.

"I am not good at handling emotion—I mean deep emotion—like... loving you.

Fact is—I'm afraid to love you. That seems backwards, but in my head it's the biggest challenge for me.

See—all I have some nights is just fear. My PTSD haunts me. Every little noise makes me jump. I sleep with a knife under my pillow. Never told you that, did I?"

Marlee drew close and took his hand. She nuzzled into his body on the right—where it didn't hurt.

"I feel like all my problems are just gonna fall on you and mess up your chance at happiness," he said.

"I don't see problems, Daniel! I see a man climbing out of a hole and learning to stand and walk tall again," Marlee said.

"I fear that I won't be a good husband or a good father. I don't know how to do either of those," he said.

"You can learn, Daniel. That's what marriage is for."

"What if I fail the test? Don't measure up? Can't handle being tied down?"

"Nobody's tying you down, you big buffalo!

You're not here to do what I think you should do or what I want you to do.

You're here to share your life with someone who happens to give a damn about what happens to you and whether you are happy or not.
Daniel, you have to see that you have choices and be willing to take chances to see if you can make tomorrow better than today. All your tomorrows."

He squinted at her. "Why do you care about me so damn much?
Why do you think I am worth the trouble? I don't even feel worthy of *you*, to be honest."

"I think I see you as you *are*, Daniel. Not as you see yourself in the ugly reflection of your fear and loneliness.
I see a man who is a man--and has the qualities I am looking for in a man: honesty, courage, loyalty, not afraid to work for what he wants, and a nice ass."

They both smiled and pressed against each other— hearts beating strong enough to feel it through their shirts into their souls, strong enough to know what was true and that it could be trusted.

***

It was Marlee who found out first.

Because she works in a hospital and in a small regional trauma center like Sacred Heart, news travels fast.

The police found his body around seven that morning—beside the tracks.

If it had been dark, the engineer would never had even seen him or felt the slight lurch as it slammed into the man standing on the tracks.

The Emergency Room just confirmed the cause of death and had the body send to the morgue downstairs.

Marlee arrived just as they were preparing to move him and was asked if she knew the victim: Rex Randall.

She covered her mouth as she saw Daniel's friend—both for the first and the last time.

"I know his friend he worked with during the summer out on the forest fires," she admitted.

"I don't know of any next of kin. He's ex-military so maybe the VA has a record."

The sergeant thanked her as he wrote down the information.

What will I tell Daniel? she wondered.
Maybe I could have saved him--let Daniel bring him home to sleep on the couch.

Oh, how terrible!
Her feelings were a turbulent mix of both relief, and guilt.

Later that evening she broke the news.
"I'm so sorry, Daniel. I feel responsible."

"Not your fault. Hopefully he was hammered out of his mind and didn't feel a thing," Daniel said.

"I prayed for the best outcome for him—but I didn't expect *this!*" Marlee said.

"I prayed for him too," Daniel said.
"I asked the Lord to show mercy and forgiveness to Rex. In the end, I just said: 'Thy Will be done'.

But this is not how I thought it would turn out.

I guess God has a better plan for Rex--in Heaven."

Marlee threw her arms around Daniel's neck and buried her face in his neck. A little sob came from her throat.

Just as she was falling off to sleep Daniel lifted her in his powerful arms and carried her upstairs.

Somewhere on their street a piano could be heard in someone's house, playing a sweet passage in a Beethoven sonata that lingered like the scent of lilacs in the air.

Chapter Fifteen   No Safe Haven

It is a frightening fact that hospitals in the U.K. and the United States are becoming unsafe—not because of contagion or personnel shortages, although those exist.

It is because the level of violence that patients and visitors direct at hospital nurses, staff, and doctors has risen exponentially in recent years.

Nurses and intake workers are assaulted, spit on, slapped and attacked on a regular basis. While authorities blame drug abuse and homelessness, very little is being done about it on a system-wide basis.

Often only after tragedy strikes, do those who control the purse-strings act and install security personnel and protocols.

Tuesday was the day Sacred Heart Medical Center & Children's Hospital managed to earn a spot in the evening news.

Two—possibly more—armed men in disguise stormed the hospital pharmacy in broad daylight.

What they were after wasn't just the contents of the cash register; they were after opioids, narcotics, and painkillers of every kind—other than aspirin.
They callously gunned down the lone security guard who tried to stop them.

Marlee was safely out of harm's way on the seventh floor in a consulting room when Code Black was announced. 'Black' for invasion by terrorists, robbers, criminals.
The very thought was paralyzing.

"What do we do?" asked the intern in alarm.
"Lockdown," said Marlee.

Footsteps could be heard running in the hall, which was contrary to protocol and only scared the crap out of everybody on the 7th Floor—which was a Psychiatry facility and kind of scary all on its own.

Marlee called Security but got a recorded message.
She then called the Front Desk but her call went to voicemail.
So she called Daniel.

"Daniel? Something is happening and I can't find out what…" but he cut her off.

"It's on the news. An armed robbery at your pharmacy. Where are you?" he demanded.

"I'm locked down on Seven. With my intern. What do I do?"

"Stay put. *Do not* move! Where's Security in that place?"

"I don't know. Nobody is picking up."

"Stay right where you are, Marlee. I'm going to come and get you. Just give me some time to get in there. Okay?"

"Okay, Daniel. Don't do something...dumb, okay?"

Daniel now was a licensed Private Investigator and carried a pistol everywhere. He often practiced at the range to improve his aim and response times.

Marlee was worried that he would use his gun if the situation called for it—she *knew* him-- and knew he could react as his Airforce training had taught him to.

He could shoot to kill without blinking an eye.

Where are the police? she wondered.

All was still on the 7th Floor now and that was unnerving.

Where is everybody?

It seemed like an eternity but suddenly there were voices outside. Someone called her name through the door.

It was a police officer, a hospital administrator—and Daniel!

She opened and rushed into Daniel's arms.

"Dr. McCowan? Are you alone?"

Her young female intern then fled through the door and the administrator and the policeman took her down the elevator.

"You didn't shoot anybody on the way in?" Marlee said looking up into his face with a weak smile.

"Didn't have to," he said. "The place is crawling with cops."

"I may as well have been on the Moon up here," Marlee said. "No idea what was going on--on the Ground Floor."

"It's good you missed it," said Daniel with a snort. "Like a Dodge City bank robbery in 1885! Guard was killed and pharmacy people roughed up by these thugs—whoever they were."

"Take me home." Marlee slipped into a jacket and locked the room behind her.

"The back way," she said. "It's stairs that lead to the back parking where my car is."

"Leave it tonight. Mine's in 'Visitor'. Don't want it towed," he said.

***

"I don't like it," Daniel said. "I don't like it at all!
Let's get you a gun that you can handle—like a small Smith & Wesson. They make guns for women now, with comfortable grips and balance, and lots of American women are packing them."

"I don't think we have to go that far yet, Daniel. I'm a doctor for gawd's sake—not John Wayne. I'm afraid that when the time came to pull the trigger--I would flinch."

"That's why you need training. We train that hesitancy out of you. You do the job; as the old Western heroes used to say: 'Shoot first—ask questions afterward."

"Can we talk about something else. This makes me nervous. Can we order in Chinese or something? I'm not in the mood to cook."

After dinner they curled up with a drink on the couch.

"The way I look at it," Daniel began, "we can do one of two things.

We can have a security system installed here in your place—cameras, motion detectors—the whole nine yards.

Or two—you could have an on-site security person who will check doors and windows every night, maintain an attitude of vigilance to detect any unusual behavior or events, and serve as a personal bodyguard to protect you in any situation."

Daniel looked at Marlee.

"And give you really good backrubs after a long day at work." He grinned.

"Oh, I see! So you are inviting yourself over on a permanent basis, is that it?"

Marlee twisted slightly to face him with a mischievous look.

"'Two can live as cheaply as one' my mom used to say," said Daniel.

"You know—that's the first time you ever said anything about your mother. I know you lost her. What was it like at home when you were a kid?"

"Oh gosh, now we are getting off-topic altogether. I can speak about that another time.
Right now I want to know--do I waste another month's rent on that ratty apartment?
Or do I pack up and move uptown with a beautiful lady that I like a lot!"

"Just *like*?" Marlee teased.

"That information is confidential," Daniel said. "I can only release it under certain conditions."

"Let me guess…when you and this lady are snuggled under the covers on a moonlit night?" she said.

"That could do it," he said.

He pulled her to him and kissed her hard.

"That could definitely do it," he said.

***

Daniel had three messages: on from an attorney he met recently, and two from a police investigator working a big arson case that was connected to some fires down in Wenatchee.

Arson is usually either a crime of revenge or for insurance money.

The attorney was representing a client whose insurance payout had been denied on the grounds of suspicion of arson for fraudulent purposes.

He hired Daniel to find out whether someone else had been responsible for these fires in town.

That idea fit with what the Wenatchee Fire Department investigators were saying.

That there was a rash of fires set by people --who ranged from pure nutcases to people with gang connections that spread all over the state—and that included Spokane.

What local and state police needed was information.

The only way to get it was put your nose in where it doesn't belong and tap street informants who knew who was doing what to whom and for how much.

Or put your finger on someone legit—an expert in the field or law enforcement.

Turns out that Travis Drum—a recent high school graduate with some experience with arson in his hometown a hundred-fifty miles southwest of Spokane--was just the man.

"I've been on the trail of a number of persons of interest in Wenatchee," Travis said.

"Some of them I actually know by name. But it's the hidden mastermind in the background that make this work very dangerous, Daniel."

Travis was working his way up to being a state-licensed arson investigator and he was a smart kid.

"So help me get a handle on what the Big Picture is, Travis," said Daniel. "Let's sort out the amateurs from the pros."

Over pizza, the two investigators went through several years of casefiles that were both still under investigation in Wenatchee and had been shared with Daniel by Spokane's Finest—both in law enforcement and in fire protection.

By the time Marlee rolled in, the living room looked like Operation Central for a military campaign.

"Meet Travis Drum, honey. He's a gold mine for me right now."

"Nice to meet you," said Travis, a tall, good-looking boy with eyes that looked right at you.

"Nice to meet you too, Travis. Are you staying in town long?" Marlee started to tidy up the pizza crusts and boxes and offered dessert.

"We're going to be a while longer, Marlee," Daniel said. "You go on up to bed whenever you like."

She left the two men murmuring and pointing at the pile of maps and papers that were the subject of their interest.

At length Daniel said: "Okay, let's park it here. You keep working on this guy McBride at your end, and I'll keep working on the men he seems to be connected to here in Spokane.

We'll do it like a bridge—we'll meet in the middle. We have to have enough evidence to show the District Attorney that he or she's got a case to prosecute.

And we have to get it very carefully because if anyone gets wind of it, they're as good as gone," said Daniel.

"Copy that, Mr. Briar."

"Actually it's Sgt. Briar. Or it was. Retired airforce. You been in the service?"

"No," Travis said. "Still on my to-do list."

"Sure. Keep your wits about you. I have a feeling this is gonna bust wide open soon. Mostly thanks to you and your team."

They shook hands and Travis piled into his pickup and disappeared into the night.

Crickets were chirping and the odd bat was swooping low for the mosquitoes coming up from the ponds and pools of the Spokane River about a mile and a half downhill from where he was standing.

True to his word, he checked every window and door before retiring. He hadn't got around to the cameras yet, but that could wait.

Right now the woman in his life was brushing her teeth upstairs—and *that* couldn't wait!

***

Marlee called first.

"Mom? Can I come over? I have been too busy with everything lately. I feel bad like I've been neglecting you."

"You *have* been—ever since that Daniel moved in with you. You never have time for me."

Doris chuckled. "Of course you can. Bring something tasty for our snack."

They greeted each other warmly.

Marlee's Mom had made the kitchen so cozy over the years: lace curtains, little jars of stuff on every shelf. Flowers in mason jars and a smell of baking that never quite goes away.

"I feel 100%, dear," Doris said. "Like I was never sick a day in my life. Not like your poor father."

"That's so good to hear, Mom. You are all the family I have left. I wished for the longest time to have had my sister longer, but I guess it wasn't meant to be."

"I wanted it different too, Marlee. Believe me.

Let's make some coffee. I might have some rum to put in it—somewhere...here.

You didn't just come to talk about the past, dear. Tell about your Daniel, and your work."

Doris was clearly avoiding the topic.

"Did I tell you about the robbery and shooting at work?" said Marlee.

"Oh my Heaven's no! Was anybody hurt? When was this?"

"Tuesday, Mom. I was up in the Psych Wing and I only heard about it when I called Daniel who told me it was on the news. I never listen to the radio at work."
Marlee filled her in on the other details.

"Are you sure you are safe at that place?" said Doris. "PBS had a documentary on rising violence at healthcare facilities."

"Tell me about it," said Marlee.

"Look, Mom, they've offered me a promotion. A big one—a gamechanger."

She related to her Mom about the position as Acting Head of Psychiatry and what that would entail.

She looked at her mother.
"Whaddya think?"

"Well it is flattering that after just a short time at the hospital they think you are the right person for the job.
Can you handle it, Marlee? And in light of this business with robbery and shooting, do you think this is the right environment for you?"

"That's what I'm not sure of," Marlee said. "The workload will be crushing and although the pay is good, I still want to have some time for me—for a life apart from being a child psychiatrist."

"You're thinking about Daniel, aren't you?"

"I am sure about him, Mom—and for the first time since we met, I think he's sure about me."

"So if you decide to be a wife, you are thinking about children as well I imagine," Doris said.

"I'm ready for it, Mom. I mean I'm ready for marriage and motherhood.
I didn't have a man in my life when I started my career. Then the whole thing with Jarrod came up and then crashed and burned.
I was thinking I don't need marriage or even a relationship—not if I'm going to get shit on like that."

"I understand, dear. You certainly didn't deserve that. And for what it's worth—I don't think that was a failure on your part to see it coming. He was just a sneaky bastard. I hope he gets what he deserves."

For one brief moment Marlee wanted to let her in on what Ricki had said.

"I have concerns about Daniel because he is now working in a risky situation—I mean, what else is new?
Firefighting gets him into the hospital after a freakin' tree falls on him!
But now he carries a gun—that tells me a lot about being a PI. I don't like it. He wants me to carry a gun. Isn't that nuts?"

Doris poured another dribble of rum into her coffee.
"Maybe not as nuts as it sounds, Marlee.
Spokane is not the safest town in America. I stayed because your father got a good job after the Depression was over and we had two kids and it never occurred to us to go anywhere else.

My generation isn't like your generation—working online, traveling all the time, moving to one job—then another. All on contract."

"I just don't know what to say about the promotion. I haven't even told Daniel."

"Well just let it settle in your mind, dear. I know you will make the right decision.

You always have."

Chapter Sixteen   Is there a Plan B?

"You know I'll be the *last* person to try to put the brakes on, Daniel. But sometimes I feel that the walls are closing in around us.

The fact that you pack a gun and that you want me to pack one too tells me that things aren't right somehow. Am I making sense here?"

"It's just a precaution, honey. Okay? A woman alone is not safe and if you had a handgun it would even the playing field."

Daniel had his feet up and was resting a beer on his belly.

"Guess what? I got an offer for a promotion!"

Marlee told him about the new position in a positive way, highlighting the status and salary and potential for a permanent place in a prominent medical center in Eastern Washington.

"But...?" Daniel was no fool. He knew there was a 'but'.

"But I wonder if this is where we should spend the rest of our lives. We both have transferrable credentials.

We could live in California or on the Oregon coast. Some nice small towns down there," Marlee was saying.

"I sense there is something deep going on with you, Marlee.

It's me, isn't it? I've turned things upside down for you."

"No, I mean—yes, I mean—I am still really rattled by this robbery at work and it makes me think where this is all going.

I talked to Doris. She is happy to move somewhere safer if we decide that is what we want."

"You want her to live with us?"

"That's not what I'm saying. I actually didn't think of it that way.

I just mean if we got married and had kids, is this the best place to raise a family?"

"I don't mind if Doris lives with us," said Daniel.

Marlee's jaw must have dropped because Daniel then said: "No. I'm serious. She's getting on and we could afford a bigger house."

"I just want to initiate the conversation with you, Daniel. I think we have to plan the next ten years—or at least talk about it."

"Alright. I am totally in agreement with that. Thing is--right now I have this massive criminal investigation into an arson ring that is going to take all my time.

I have to drive down to Wenatchee to meet Travis and his people tomorrow and won't be back until Sunday night."

"Oh. I thought we would take in a movie." Marlee couldn't hide her disappointment.

"I'm sorry. I'll make it up to you. I promise, Marlee."

He gathered her in his arms and that always had a magical calming effect on Marlee--as if she could face anything—so long as his strong arms and tender caresses were there when she needed them.

***

It is a uplifting day's drive--from Spokane to Wenatchee on the eastern slope of the

Cascades. The full grandeur of Washington State is on display—its magnificent mountains and valleys, farms and forests, the sheer vastness of the Pacific Northwest is open to view.

The Apple Capital is a thriving town by the mighty Columbia River that is one of America's safest and most enjoyable places to live.

This was all running through Daniel's head as he met up with young Travis Drum at his office in the fire station just north of the town of Wenatchee.

Sure, there was crime—burglary, drugs, prostitution, robbery, but on a scale of one to ten, Wenatchee was about a one, Travis had said.

Which made the series of arsons that had plagued this quiet town a *mystery*.

Travis Drum was part of a growing band of investigators who were pulling the noose around the neck of organized crime in Washington State.

"Meet the team," said Travis, inviting Daniel to be seated at the table.

There were seasoned firefighters, state police, detectives from Seattle and San Francisco—a whole slate of serious men and women who were determined to end this problem.

The problem extended to Spokane and that is why Daniel was here.

An officer was running a projector and the lights dimmed.

"Here is closed circuit TV footage of two commercial fires that we determined to be arson," she said.

She paused to focus on two men and a white truck in the parking lot who showed up to watch both buildings—one a lumberyard and one a retail store—go up in smoke.

"We have identified both guys," she continued, "and we have a make and plate on the truck. Neither are local and both have ties to this group or gang we are after."

Another officer stood up and said that this network of crime included bikers and drug dealers who were branching out to other areas where illegal income was to be had.

Contract murder was at the top of that list.

But some clever crook realized there was money in setting fires too.

The general consensus of the investigating team was that they could bring this whole thing down if they thwarted and captured key players—the ringleader, the money men.

"What is the connection to Spokane?" Daniel asked.

"There is a small gang that does the bidding of a corrupt attorney who himself has ties to bigger fish in bigger cities.
If we can get our hands on this guy and put the squeeze on him, I think we can solve a bunch of crimes—including the arson."

"You got a description of this attorney?" Daniel said.
"Better! We got a name and a photo."

An 8½ by 11 glossy was passed to Daniel.
It showed a man younger and better-looking than what he was expecting.
"Kennedy. Jarrod Kennedy," said the officer.

"Don't know him," said Daniel. "It won't be easy to put together a case unless we got credible witness testimony. I know for damn sure he's not the one lighting the match!"

"That's why we need you, Daniel," said Travis. "You're our guy in Spokane. You have your finger on the pulse of the town. It's not a hell of a lot bigger than Wenatchee and somebody has to know something."

"Copy that," said Daniel. "Travis, can you give me a brief rundown of some of the cases so I can form an impression of the M.O. and types of victims we are seeing."

He did not mention that he had been hired by a Spokane attorney to exonerate a certain client from an arson that recently happened.

Daniel was with Travis until suppertime.

He stopped at a burger joint on the way out of town and didn't get back to Spokane until the moon was fairly high in the sky and the sun a mere smudge of orange over the distant Cascades to the west.

***

Much of a private investigator's work is done by computer, so Daniel spent most of the next day trying to find out more about the lawyer's client accused of setting fire—or having someone set fire—to a brand new housing tract under construction just outside of town.

The guy was an investor who was involved with a developer and from there the picture got quite murky.

But one of names that also came up on the screen, though, was that of a local criminal lawyer: Jarrod Kennedy.

Who is this guy? Daniel shifted his focus and decided this guy needed a stakeout.

Surveillance is the core skill of a PI and Daniel was still learning. He rented an old shitbox car that nobody would notice sitting on the street.

He had different cameras with zoom lenses and night vision and he was pretty good with them.

By midweek, he had a file on Kennedy thicker than the menu at Rocky's Diner.

If he could just catch this guy in the act—whatever the act was—he might get closer to his goal.

If he could show the investor was set-up by Kennedy to take the fall for a fire that earned the developer a few million in insurance payouts...if!

He read the statements of the investor that his attorney had on file.

He staked out Kennedy—and discovered the cops had a man on him as well.

Then Daniel got lucky.

One of the two men from the Wenatchee fire scene photo the police had was on the street right here in Spokane--talking to Kennedy in a not very pleasant manner—giving Daniel time to snap several photos that were clearly incriminating for both of them.

If they could put all this evidence under the nose of the new and feisty lady District Attorney, there might be a hope for an arrest or two.

Two birds with one stone, Daniel muttered under his breath.

As it turned out, the DA *did* put two-and-two together and issued a warrant for Kennedy, the developer, and the thug by week's end.

Daniel took all this to his client—who was thrilled to have enough grounds to have the charges against the investor dropped--and gave Daniel a nice fat check to show his appreciation.

"It all came down to this lawyer Kennedy," Daniel was saying with a mouthful at dinner with Marlee.

"Kennedy? Jarrod Kennedy?"
"Yeah, that's him. You don't know this guy do you? Tell me you don't know this guy!

He's up to his ass in indictments and once the judge is finished with him, he's not gonna see the light of day for thirty years."

Marlee was in shock. She just sat there.

"Jarrod Kennedy was my fiancé a year ago," she said through her teeth. "He dumped me for some little ho.
I was quite a mess—not because he was Mr. Right, but because he cheated me in every way that mattered. I hope he fucking burns!"

"Considering he has been arrested for his control of an arson ring, that's an appropriate choice of words," Daniel said; and then he paused.

"Now it's my turn to be blown away—you were engaged to this prick?
Let's leave it where it belongs, Marlee—in the *past!*
He can't hurt you now so let it go. Please, Marlee! I love you!"

Chapter Seventeen   Make Or Break

Something was on her mind.

It had less to do with Jarrod than the fact that Daniel was now battling with the underworld of crime and corruption.

It was no surprise that Jarrod Kennedy was involved in such things. That was his nature.

But how to protect the man I love? was the question.

"I won't lie to you, Daniel. I'm worried. No—I'm scared. What if these men come after you?"

"I have to admit that same thought crossed my mind," Daniel replied. "Good reason to put the security cameras in--finally."

"I really hate to say this, but I don't think this kind of work is right for you, Daniel.

And I know I've said it a thousand times, but I can easily support us on my salary.

Especially if I take this promotion.

You won't have to work at all. You can stay home and build boats. Fill the basement with lumber and carpentry tools."

"You feel pretty strongly about this don't you?" Daniel said.

"I want a life with you Daniel! I don't want to be holding my head down when we're out in public in case some gangster sees you.

I don't want to worry if you will come home at night or if I will have to see you in the ER—like Rex—covered by a white sheet that matches the color of your pallid dead body!
I don't!!"

"I get that, Marlee. I forgot you had to ID Rex that day. I'm sorry for that.
Listen. Here's what I'm going to do.

I'm going to get in touch with my CO from my old squad--who is working down at Vandenberg AFB--and see if he has any work there for me.
They always need experienced people in the Air Force. I have no clue what I could do for them but Colonel Thomas will.
It's worth a shot. What do you think?"

"Try it. Yes! Call him up or whatever. Just something where nobody has a gun pointed at your back!"

***

Marlee called her mother to talk again about leaving Spokane.

Doris simply said *'Come over, I need to talk to you.'*

That wasn't like Doris.

Maybe it was good that this Jarrod thing had come up—it pushed Marlee to be ready for anything.

But what Doris had to say--Marlee was *not* ready for.

"I've always hated guns. That's why I wouldn't let your father own one."

Doris was seated at the kitchen table, a cup of tea in a real china teacup on a china saucer.

"So I don't blame you one bit for pressuring Daniel to change his job. I don't want him to end up like Ranee."

"What do you mean, Mom?"

The story of her younger sister's death was a taboo topic—even while her Father lived. It was no doubt a contributing factor to his early demise.

"You were too young, too innocent to, Marlee," Doris went on. "It was a shame that fell on us all, regardless of what really happened.

It has been a pain I could never soothe but I want to tell you in hopes that it might ease your own pain.

Because I know you suffered, Marlee!"

Marlee had carried the burden of her sister's strange death--without knowing what had really happened—long after she left for college.

'A tragic accident' was all she was told.

Doris carefully unfolded a yellowed piece of paper and spread it with her bony fingers on the table. It was handwritten.

Marlee realized it was written by her younger sister Ranee.

"After she was gone, we found this in her room," Doris said. "It seems to be a suicide note, although that is not how she died."

Marlee's heart stopped.

"She was murdered, Marlee.

By a man with a gun. 'Killed in self-defense' said the police.

But it's more complicated than that."

"Go on," said Marlee shaking from head to toe.

"If you read the letter you see how upset Ranee was...about something that had happened to her.
Something that took from her the desire to live, to go on living with the pain of whatever it was.
You see that she never said *what* in this letter.
Just words like 'I don't belong in this world' and 'I feel so hopeless and useless'.
For a time, we understood she was depressed and wanted to take her life."

Doris looked at her hands while massaging them--as arthritics do.

"How she ended up in that man's room I do not know.
From what the police told me it appeared that she had gone there with a gun—to even the score or right some wrong done to her.

She shot that man! But she sustained a bullet wound in return--that cost her life.

What I think is, Marlee--she was raped and wanted to end it all but then decided she would confront the man who did it.

She couldn't deal with it, Marlee. This letter was written only a week before the incident. I never showed it to the police or anybody else except your father."

Tears spattered the paper as Marlee tried to hear her baby sister's cry for help in the words written there.

She pulled her mother's chair next to hers and threw her arms around the woman who had lived with this and never spoken of this until now.
A mother who had lost her baby in such a brutal way, a senseless way.
Her mother.

Marlee wondered if the reason she became a doctor, a psychiatrist--was to assuage her unconscious guilt and shame for not being there for her sister at the only time she was really needed.

Then maybe this letter would not have been written, and Ranee would have had options instead of--instead of doing what she did that terrible night!

Darkness crept into the room as the sun slipped into some distant ocean, bringing light to the other side of the world and leaving none to comfort two women wrapped in a tight embrace in the still of evening.

***

Daniel left one voice message on her cell. Then another.

Finally she texted him that he should sleep—she was spending the night with her Mom.

It was hard not to--but he resisted. Whatever it was—it would keep. He knew Marlee needed her privacy as much as he did.

"Every year on her birthday I go her little spot in Memorial Gardens and leave a little bouquet of daisies," said Doris.

Breakfast was on the table but neither of them had much appetite.

"This time—take me! I never even knew where she was laid to rest. That hurt more than anything.

I could only kneel in church and ask that she be at peace, forgiven of sin and worthy of God's blessings."

"That's good, Marlee!" Doris said. "That is as much as anyone could do for her.

Taken at fourteen, I never blamed God—I know better. But I blamed myself more than anything."

"Would you be willing to come to church with me? We could offer a prayer together!"

Marlee then said:

"*We* are still *here*, Mom. And I don't believe Ranee would want this to go on anymore.

Let's seek healing in The Holy Spirit. Let's ask for that."

Marlee turned to her mother. "Will you go with me?"

"I want Daniel to come," Doris said.

"He will. I know he will," said Marlee.

Chapter Eighteen   California Dreaming

It was Daniel. He never called her at work unless it was important.

"I got a response, Marlee!
"Remember I wrote my old Commanding Officer about getting work with him at Vandenberg?
Damned if he didn't write back! He said there's plenty of work on the base and former veterans have preference.

He said there's two ways to do this: one is hire me on as a civilian contractor for the Air Education & Training Command 30th Operations Group—where *he* is.

The other—and I wanna hear your thoughts on this—is he *orders* me to appear for duty, he *calls me up* to active duty as a non-commissioned flight instructor.
That way I get my old rank re-instated with salary and benefits from the Air Force.
In fact, he wants me to come back as a Senior NCO at the Master Sergeant E-7 grade.

This is a dream come true for us, Marlee!"

272

"So let me get this straight--you are going to be in the Air Force again—on active duty? Are you ready for that, Daniel Briar?" she said.

"Given the current situation, I am more than ready to get out of the detective business, and get out of this town--which has suddenly become very claustrophobic."

"I think you should go for it, Daniel. Re-enlist and cash in on your service to your country cause you've already paid those dues!"

"This is California, Marlee! Imagine! Santa Barbara is on the magnificent Pacific coast with year-round surfing and a lifestyle that could only be Southern California!"

Marlee was laughing with delight.

"I can't wait! Wait till I tell Doris! Send that response right now, Daniel Briar!

I will prepare a letter for the hospital announcing my resignation with two weeks notice."

"I love you, Marlee!" Daniel said. "We can investigate getting you a job on the base under the Military Spouse Preference category. I'm sure the Air Force could use a good psychiatrist there."

"Except for one small detail you silly man," she replied.

"What's that?"

"I am not your spouse yet. You forgot to ask me to marry you!"

"Marry me, Marlee! Marry me this week!"

"I would prefer to do this in person. I want you on bended knee holding out a big fat diamond ring and telling me this will be forever."

"I'm on the way to Spence's Jewellers right now!" he announced. "I'll pick you up at work at five."

Then he remembered the license. *Get the license first, dummy!*

It was only a matter of filling out the form and paying the fee to the clerk.

Daniel stuffed the license in his jacket pocket and raced down the street to the jewelry store.

"It's only 0.75 carats but the ring is 18K."

Daniel had the big black Dodge door open on the passenger side and people were gazing and covering their mouths because he was down on one knee to the lady in the white lab coat who seemed to be part of the hospital staff!

But what were they doing out in the parking lot? A small crowd had gathered.

"Will you—Marlee McCowan—be my wife? To have and to hold, through richer and poorer, in sickness and health, in Washington and California--and anyplace else on this Earth that we choose to live for the rest of our lives?"

The lady in the lab coat was beaming and the way the slanting sun caught her face made her so utterly exquisitely lovely that some in the crowd gasped and held their breath...

...to see what she would answer!

"I will," she said--and the collective sigh of the impromptu audience could be heard to faintly echo off the East Wing wall!
They began applauding as this handsome, strapping fellow slipped the gold band with its radiant stone onto her left hand --and then rose to his full height like a god from the sea.

And...kissed her! Kissed her with a kiss that only sea-gods or great heroes can give to the goddess lucky enough to be held in his embrace.

***

"Oh, my dear!" said Doris holding Marlee's hand to admire the engagement ring. "When shall we set the date for? August?"

"Saturday," said Marlee.
"I've already spoken to the pastor. Twelve noon. Now you have to help me find a gown!"

"Oh my Lord above," Doris exclaimed. "I feel like I'm in a whirlwind romance--like those stories—you know?"

"Well this one definitely requires your presence, Mom. I have to call Bev to see if she'll be my bridesmaid.
I have to get my hair done, my nails done. What have I forgotten?"

Marlee and her mother were chatting away in the living room while Daniel was on his cell outside on the front porch.

"Hey! Travis! How's it going?
You're getting married?! That's awesome, man!
Ah, as a matter of fact—so am I! What are you doing this weekend?"

So Travis agreed to be Best Man and would drive up from Wenatchee with his new girlfriend.

The pastor had said--all they needed was a license and two witnesses!

And God's blessings, thought Marlee. "*That is what makes happy endings!*

The End

If you enjoyed this story, check for more Mason Stone stories on Amazon.com/Mason Stone or Indigo.ca

Or ask for them in your local bookstore.

www.ingramcontent.com/pod-product-compliance
Lightning Source LLC
Chambersburg PA
CBHW021440070526
44577CB00002B/221